GENDER IDENTITY

Beyond Pronouns and Bathrooms

Maria Cook

Illustrated by Alexis Cornell

Titles in the Inquire & Investigate
Social Issues of the Twentieth Century set

Check out more titles at www.nomadpress.net

Nomad Press
A division of Nomad Communications
10 9 8 7 6 5 4 3 2 1

This book was manufactured by Versa Press,
East Peoria, Illinois
April 2019, Job #J18-13161

ISBN Softcover: 978-1-61930-759-9
ISBN Hardcover: 978-1-61930-756-8

Educational Consultant, Marla Conn

Questions regarding the ordering of this book should be addressed to
Nomad Press
2456 Christian St.
White River Junction, VT 05001
www.nomadpress.net

Gender Identity: Beyond Pronouns and Bathrooms is one of the easiest to read and most interesting books on gender and the history of transgender pioneers that I have sat down with. Maria Cook has done a brilliant job of capturing the important moments and the key leaders in the transgender movement, as well as providing an understanding of the nuance of language and the issues. For anyone who is transgender, who knows someone who is transgender, or simply wants to learn about the transgender movement, this is the book for you. I love the use of illustrations by Alexis Cornell as well as the helpful callouts that are used to bring out the important points. We are at an important crossroads in terms of widening our moral compass, and the arrival of this book is timely and very useful reading for leaders and allies everywhere. It is an especially important read for anyone who is currently struggling with their gender.

I was America's first-ever major party candidate for governor who is also transgender. I am fortunate to live in the state of Vermont, where strong protections are in place for transgender individuals. Unfortunately, that is not the case everywhere. In many parts of the world, being transgender can be a death sentence. That said, there has been tremendous progress in America during the last few decades. Transgender leaders are now showing up routinely in politics and industry. Schools are by and large supportive and inclusive. At press time, 20 states have transgender protections built into law. My state just passed a gender-neutral bathroom bill. We also have been able to choose the bathroom that matches our gender identity for many years.

I recognize that my success has been the result of thousands of Vermonters before me who have fought for what is right and what is just. That is why I ran for governor. I am riding on the shoulders of the many people before me, and I hope my work will further enable people after me. It is so important that we work hard to become the authentic people we really are. For those of you who may be currently struggling with your gender identity, I hope this book helps you to accomplish your goals and that you can ultimately experience the freedom and joy that authenticity provides. I promise you the work that you are doing is very important. For those who know someone who is struggling, this book will help you with the language and understanding necessary to become a helpful ally.

I know that it can be difficult to maintain a positive outlook when we are fighting for the justice our community deserves. I know it can be hard when we see leaders such as our president trying to reverse the gains we have achieved. However, as Maria Cook points out, in capturing our history in this book, the light of justice will shine brightly and prevail over the darkness of division. That is why the LGBTQ movement was formed. We know that when one community is targeted, no community is safe. We all must stand together to ensure justice for all. This book affirms that we are going to continue to move forward. I hope that it gives you the confidence to personally take the steps you need to move forward. I will also tell you that nothing is impossible when you are on the side of justice.

—**Christine Hallquist,**
the first openly transgender major party
gubernatorial nominee in the United States

You can use a smartphone or tablet app to scan the QR codes and explore more! Cover up neighboring QR codes to make sure you're scanning the right one. You can find a list of URLs on the Resources page.

If the QR code doesn't work, try searching the internet with the Keyword Prompts to find other helpful sources.

 gender identity

Interested in primary sources? **Look for this icon.**

PS

What are source notes?

In this book, you'll find small numbers at the end of some paragraphs. These numbers indicate that you can find source notes for that section in the back of the book. Source notes tell readers where the writer got their information. This might be a news article, a book, or another kind of media. Source notes are a way to know that what you are reading is information that other people have verified. They can also lead you to more places where you can explore a topic that you're curious about!

Contents

Glossary ▼ Resources ▼ Index

TIMELINE

1930................................. Lili Elbe becomes the first recorded person to medically transition.

1933................................. Lili Elbe's biography, *Man Into Woman*, is published, bringing some of the first widespread attention to transgender people.

1950................................. Christine Jorgensen becomes the second recorded person and first American to medically transition, with help from notes taken during Lili Elbe's 1930 and 1931 procedures.

1964................................. Reed Erickson founds the Erickson Educational Foundation to fund research about transgender people and open the first North American gender clinic at Johns Hopkins University.

1965................................. Vanguard, the first gay youth organization in the United States, is formed in San Francisco.

1966................................. Fighting breaks out between police officers and LGBTQ patrons of Compton's Cafeteria in the Tenderloin neighborhood of San Francisco, California, in what would become known as the Compton Cafeteria Riot.

1969................................. The Stonewall Riots take place at the Stonewall Inn in New York City and protests continue for weeks afterward.

1970................................. Sylvia Rivera and Marsha P. Johnson form STAR (Street Transvestite Action Revolutionaries) to help LGBTQ youth in New York—particularly transgender and nonbinary youth.

1972................................. Sweden becomes the first country to allow people to legally change their gender.

1973................................. An anti-cross-dressing ordinance, which had been in place since 1851, is struck down in Chicago, Illinois.

1975................................. Minneapolis, Minnesota, becomes the first U.S. city to pass an ordinance protecting transgender people from discrimination.

1980................................ Germany passes a law that makes it legal for transgender people to change their gender on legal documents, but only after sex-reassignment surgery.

1985................................ Lou Sullivan, who brought public awareness to the fact that transgender men could be gay, publishes *Information for the Female-To-Male Crossdresser and Transsexual*, the first guidebook for transgender men.

1992................................ The first International Conference on Transgender Law and Employment Policy is held in Houston, Texas.

1993................................ A 21-year-old transgender man named Brandon Teena is murdered in Nebraska, in a case that would capture national attention.

1998................................ A 34-year-old African American transgender woman named Rita Hester is murdered in Massachusetts.

1999................................ Transgender woman and activist Gwendolyn Ann Smith holds the first Transgender Day of Remembrance to honor the memory of Rita Hester and all other victims of deadly anti-transgender violence.

2002................................ The Transgender Law Center, a legal advocacy organization for transgender people, opens in California.

2004................................ San Francisco holds the first Trans March, its largest transgender pride parade.

2014................................ Laverne Cox becomes the first openly transgender person to appear on the cover of *Time* magazine and also the first openly transgender person to be nominated for an Emmy Award in the acting category.

2018................................ The World Health Organization re-classifies gender dysphoria as a sexual health condition rather than a mental illness.

IMPORTANT PEOPLE

Lili Elbe (1882–1931) was a Danish, transgender woman who, in 1930, became the first recorded person to medically transition. Lili was able to live publicly as a woman during a time when most people were completely unaware of the existence of transgender people. Lili's biography, *Man Into Woman*, was published in 1933. Her story also inspired a fictionalized novel, *The Danish Girl*, in 2000. A movie by the same name was released in 2015.

Christine Jorgensen (1926–1989) was a transgender woman who was the second recorded person and the first recorded American to medically transition. Some describe Christine as the first transgender celebrity, since she was a performer who talked openly about being transgender. Speaking about herself and the doctors who helped her transition, Christine once famously said, "We didn't start the sexual revolution but I think we gave it a good kick in the pants!"

Sylvia Rivera (1951–2002) was a Latina, LGBTQ, gender non-conforming activist in the early days of the LGBTQ rights movement. She participated in protests and other demonstrations throughout the 1960s, 1970s, and 1980s. Along with her friend, Marsha P. Johnson, Sylvia helped found STAR (Street Transvestite Action Revolutionaries), which helped clothe, feed, and shelter young LGBTQ people in New York City.

Marsha P. Johnson (1945–1992) was an African American, gender non-conforming LGBTQ activist in the early days of the LBGTQ rights movement. She participated in protests and demonstrations, including the famous Stonewall Riots in New York City, throughout the 1960s, 1970s and 1980s. She cofounded STAR (Street Transvestite Action Revolutionaries) along with her friend, Sylvia Rivera, in 1970.

Lou Sullivan (1951–1991) was a gay transgender man and LGBTQ activist. During the 1980s, Lou brought attention to the fact that transgender people could be gay—something that many people did not believe to be possible. Lou also wrote the first guidebook specifically for transgender men and cofounded an organization for transgender men that evolved into the present-day organization, FTM International.

Laverne Cox (1972–) is an African American transgender actress and LGBTQ activist who has risen to stardom in recent years. In 2010, Laverne became the first African American transgender woman to produce and star in her own television show. In 2014, she became the first openly transgender person to be featured on the cover of *Time* magazine. That same year, Laverne became the first openly transgender person to be nominated for an Emmy Award in the acting category.

Introduction ▶

What Is Gender Identity?

REMEMBER, KIDS, THIS ISN'T A TRUE OR FALSE QUESTION. IT'S MULTIPLE CHOICE.

What does it mean to be a gender other than male or female?

Researchers have learned something that many people have known since early human history—male and female are not the only genders! As cultures around the world become more accepting of the spectrum of different genders, people are freer to identify as they feel instead of as they are assigned.

WHAT GENDER IDENTITY MEANS

Imagine that you are a girl. You know that you're a girl the same way you know what your favorite color is or what kind of music you like best—it's just something you know about yourself. Maybe you have friends who are girls, and you share much in common with them.

There's just one problem—everyone around you says you are a boy. Your parents, teachers, and even some of your friends tell you that you have certain body parts that make you a boy, no matter how much you feel that you are a girl.

This is how many transgender people feel as they grow up. For example, actress Laverne Cox was assigned the gender of male at birth, but always felt that she was a girl. We say a baby is assigned a gender when someone, usually a medical professional, labels them as a boy or girl according to their genitalia.

In an interview with *Time* magazine in 2014, Laverne explained, "I just thought that I was a girl and that there was no difference between girls and boys."[1]

Laverne felt this way even though many people around her insisted that she was a boy. Laverne's gender identity did not fit the gender that she had been assigned. Gender identity is a person's perception of their own gender, or the gender a person feels that they are. For some people, their gender identity doesn't match their sex.

Eventually, Laverne began expressing her gender identity the way that she had always wanted, by living openly as a woman. She went on to become a successful actress. She became the first openly transgender person to be nominated for a Primetime Emmy Award in acting, and the first openly transgender person to appear on the cover of *Time* magazine.

Laverne Cox on speaking tour in 2014 in Columbia, Missouri

credit: KOMUnews (CC BY 2.0)

Everyone has a gender identity. Many cultures teach that there are only two genders: male and female. However, research has made it increasingly clear that there are many other genders. Someone can be gender fluid, agender, or bigender, among others. Several countries, including Bangladesh, Germany, and New Zealand, now legally recognize the existence of more than two genders.

In *Gender Identity*, we'll learn more about what gender is and how public policies and social attitudes have shaped the way different cultures form expectations of different gender roles. Sometimes, it can be difficult to talk about gender identity, because people can feel uncomfortable discussing it. However, it's important to recognize that humans are a very varied species with lots of different ways of being.

Let's take a look at gender in the context of a few other personal and social elements, including physical sex, sexual orientation, and cultural expectations.

GENDER IDENTITY VS. PHYSICAL SEX

You might be thinking—isn't a person's gender decided by their sex? And it's true that in most cultures, a person's gender is assigned at birth based on their perceived physical sex. For example, a baby born with a penis will usually be assigned male.

In Western cultures, it has long been assumed that a person's gender identity will always align with their physical sex. People whose gender identity aligns with the gender that they were assigned at birth are called cisgender.

VOCAB LAB

There is a lot of new vocabulary in this book. Turn to the glossary in the back when you come to a word you don't understand. Practice your new vocabulary in the VOCAB LAB activities in each chapter.

Gender identity is an issue that can make some people feel uncomfortable. It's important to speak and think openly about topics such as this so bias and discrimination diminish in our society.

However, we now know that there are many ways in which a person's gender identity might not align with their physical sex. For example, a person could be male even though they were assigned female at birth because they had a vagina. Sometimes, the sexual characteristics you're born with and the secondary sex characteristics you develop, such as facial hair and breasts, don't have anything to do with the gender you feel you really are. People whose gender identity does not align with the gender they were assigned at birth are called transgender.

There are times when a person's physical sex does not allow them to be easily categorized as male or female at birth. Some babies are born with ambiguous genitalia. They might have both a penis and vagina, neither a penis nor a vagina, or reproductive organs that are structurally a mix of both. People born with these kinds of physical traits are called intersex.

GENDER IDENTITY VS. SEXUAL ORIENTATION

Sexual orientation has to do with what gender a particular person is attracted to. For example, a woman who is attracted to men is heterosexual, while a man who is attracted to other men is homosexual. There are many different sexual orientations, including bisexual, pansexual, and asexual.

> Heterosexual people are often referred to as "straight," while homosexual people are often referred to as "gay" or "lesbian."

DISCOVERING YOU'RE INTERSEX AS A TEEN

In 2008, musician Edan Atwood shared the story of her life with ABC News. Edan discovered she was intersex at age 15, when she was found to have androgen insensitivity syndrome (AIS). Because of her condition, Edan has XY chromosomes, instead of the XX chromosomes usually associated with women. She also has no uterus and undescended testes in her abdomen. The diagnosis was difficult for Edan to accept, at first. But eventually, she was able to move forward in creating a family and successful career.

She does not consider herself any less a woman just because she is intersex. "I check the box every time it comes up: male or female? Female," she told ABC News. Edan's story is a good example of how a person's physical sex can differ from their gender identity.[2]

In many cultures, there is an expectation that physical sex, gender identity, and sexual orientation always line up in a specific way. In most cultures, a person born with a vagina would be assigned the gender of female and be expected to be attracted to men. We now know, however, that physical sex, gender identity, and sexual orientation are independent of one another—they can line up differently for different individuals.

For example, a trans woman who was incorrectly assigned the gender of male at birth due to her physical sex might be attracted to men, and therefore be heterosexual. Another trans woman may be attracted to women, and therefore be homosexual. Any individual may have any sexual orientation, regardless of their gender identity or physical sex.

Marchers at a gay pride event

GENDER IDENTITY VS. CULTURAL EXPECTATIONS

Most cultures that hold strong to the idea that male and female are the only genders usually expect men and women to differ from one another in appearance and behavior. Take a look at a magazine. Do most of the men pictured have short hair or long hair? What about the women? Are any of the men wearing skirts or high heels? Are the women wearing baseball caps? In the United States, men are generally expected to be larger, taller, and more muscular than women. Women are often expected to be more emotional, sensitive, and nurturing than men. But are these assumptions really true?

Cultural expectations can change over time. As recently as 50 years ago, men in the United States were expected to earn the majority of household income, while today, American women generally have their own careers.

But because cultural expectations still persist, people who do not conform to them often face discrimination and even physical danger. For example, several states in the United States have passed laws making it illegal for people to use restrooms that do not correspond with their documented physical sex, regardless of the person's gender identity.

This law is based on the cultural expectation that all men have particular physical traits, while all women have different physical traits.

WHAT DOES IT MEAN TO MEDICALLY TRANSITION?

Transgender people usually experience what's called "gender dysphoria," which is the feeling that their physical sex does not align with their gender identity. Because of this, many transgender people choose to medically transition. Through a variety of medical procedures, such as hormone therapy and surgery, they change certain physical traits so that their bodies more closely align with their gender identity. Not all transgender people experience gender dysphoria in the same way, and not all transgender people choose to medically transition. However, medically transitioning has been shown to improve the well-being of those transgender people who choose to pursue it.

Cultures past and present have fostered different ideas about what makes someone a certain gender, and about how people of certain genders should behave. There is evidence that certain Native American tribes, such as the Crow and Lakota, recognized three or more genders. Some modern-day countries, including Australia, Canada, and Pakistan, legally recognize a third gender in some form. Modern-day Thailand is famous for its active transgender community and is a world leader in gender-reassignment surgeries, with at least 20 medical centers able to accommodate patients undergoing the operations. However, transgender people in Thailand still struggle to be treated equally and are not able to change their gender on legal documents.

For example, this means that a trans woman, who looks like any other woman, could be forced to use the men's restroom. How do you think she would feel? How do you think the men in the bathroom would react to someone who looks like a woman using the same facility?

This could be humiliating and even dangerous. Trans men and women who are forced to use the wrong restroom have been subject to harassment. But if trans people refuse to use the wrong restrooms in states with these laws, they may face arrest.

Many people believe that cultural expectations should be relaxed so that all individuals can express their gender freely and safely.

Gender performance sometimes refers to the way men and women show their gender on a daily basis, through a variety of habits and mannerisms, in order to adhere to cultural norms. A woman shaving her legs or a man wearing a necktie could be viewed as gender performance. For transgender people, participating in the habits and behaviors associated with one's gender identity is often an important part of transitioning.

In *Gender Identity*, we'll take a closer look at some of these definitions and descriptions. We'll learn about the long history of gender identity, especially gender identities that do not conform to societal expectations, both in the United States and elsewhere in the world. From the Stonewall Riots to the institution of the Transgender Day of Remembrance, readers gain a rich understanding of how gender identity fits into culture, past and present. Let's get started!

The acronym LGBTQ stands for lesbian, gay, bisexual, transgender, queer.

● ● ● ● ● ● ● ● ● ● ● ● ☿

VOCAB LAB 📖

Write down what you think each word means. What root words can you find to help you? What does the context of the word tell you?

discrimination, **gender**, **gender fluid**, **gender identity**, **gender performance**, **intersex**, **physical sex**, **sexual orientation**, and **transgender**.

Compare your definitions with those of your friends or classmates. Did you all come up with the same meanings? Turn to the text and glossary if you need help.

KEY QUESTIONS

- How does physical sex differ from gender identity?
- Why do you think people are sometimes uncomfortable talking about gender identity?
- How does sexual orientation differ from gender identity? Is it possible for a cisgender person to have the same sexual orientation as a transgender person?

EXPLORE CULTURAL EXPECTATIONS

Cultural expectations change over time, including expectations of men and women. For example, high-heeled shoes, which are now associated with women's fashion, were originally created for men! In this activity, you'll study some cultural expectations and explore how they might have changed from past to present.

A painting of Richard Sackville by William Larkin, 1613. Check out his footwear!

- **Pick three items or behaviors that your culture associates with women.** Do some research online and at the library or a museum to discover their origins. Can you find the first instance of the items or behaviors? Why do we associate them with women?

- **Then, do the same for three items or behaviors expected of men.** Consider the following questions.

  - How did these expectations come to be?

  - How have they changed over time?

  - Was there a defining moment in history that caused the expectations to change?

- **Write about your findings and include sources.** Present what you have learned to other people and discuss your findings with one another.

To investigate more, consider items or behaviors that have always been thought of as belonging equally to men and women. Why do you think these things escaped belonging to one gender or another?

Chapter 1 ▶
Early Gender Pioneers

WE WEREN'T ALWAYS SO VISIBLE!

How did the public react to people who medically transitioned in the twentieth century?

The first transgender people who medically transitioned faced many challenges as societies had to adjust both their laws and cultural attitudes. But these first steps helped pave the way for future transgender pioneers.

Today, more people are aware of the struggles faced by transgender people, and some places are more accepting than they used to be. While there is still a long way to go before transgender people are truly treated equally, some cultural attitudes are changing for the better.

Some transgender people keep their gender a secret for a long time, even their whole lives. Why? Let's take a look.

COMING OUT

When LGBTQ people tell other people about their sexual orientation, gender identity, or both, it's called coming out. For some, coming out is something to celebrate. For others, it is a fearful and difficult process. In cultures that believe in a strict gender binary with strict roles for men and women, coming out can be especially difficult.

It can even be dangerous—in some countries, it's even illegal.

The point of coming out is that a person can be recognized for who they truly are. For some people, coming out makes it possible for them to introduce their romantic partners to family and friends, openly marry their partners, or be called by the correct pronouns, along with many other benefits.

Not everyone chooses to come out. In some cases, the potential consequences may be too great. People who come out can sometimes be excluded from their families, lose support from friends, or even lose their jobs.

Many people choose to come out in stages. For example, a person can come out to their friends before coming out to their families, or vice versa. A person might choose to come out only to those closest to them, so as not to face discrimination in certain environments, such as their workplace. There is no one correct way to take this momentous step. Different methods work for different people.

Throughout history, many cultures have resisted accepting transgender and nonbinary people. Even though transgender and nonbinary people have existed since the beginning of human history, they did not always have the opportunity to come out. However, there are a few, well-documented cases of people coming out during the past 100 years or so. Let's take a look at a couple of important figures.

BEING OUTED

Sometimes, someone who knows an LGBTQ person will spread information about that person's gender identity or sexual orientation without permission. This is called "outing" someone, and it is very harmful. Outing someone can damage their family relationships, career, or even put them in physical danger. Never share such information without permission.

GENDER WONDER

Today, the term "sex change operation" is considered outdated and offensive. Surgeries to help a person's physical sex align with their gender are now referred to as sex reassignment surgery or gender reassignment surgery. Why does language matter when talking about gender issues?"

LILI ELBE

To deadname someone is to call a person by their original name, or deadname, instead of by their chosen name. This is considered disrespectful and even offensive. This book refers to all people by their chosen names.

THE GENDER BINARY

Today, mounting evidence shows that gender is a spectrum, which includes people who are not male or female and may have more specific identities, such as bigender or gender fluid as well. Agender people do not identify as any gender. In many cultures, people who identify as a gender other than male or female still struggle for recognition and equal rights.

Lili Elbe was a transgender woman who, in 1930, became the first identifiable person to medically transition. It's possible that other people had medically transitioned before her, but Lili's case was the first to be properly documented.

Born in Vegle, Denmark, Lili was assigned the gender of male at birth. Before medically transitioning, Lili studied art at the Royal Danish Academy of Fine Arts and married a fellow painter, a woman named Gerda Gottlieb (1886–1940). Gerda worked as an illustrator for fashion magazines and books, and eventually asked Lili to be a model for some of her portraits. In order to do so, Lili had to wear women's clothing.

This experience helped affirm Lili's feeling that she was actually a woman. "I cannot deny, strange as it may sound, that I enjoyed myself in this disguise,"

A painting by Lili Elbe called *The poplars along Hobro Fjord*, 1908

Lili later wrote of the experience. "I liked the feel of soft women's clothing. I felt very much at home in them from the first moment."[1]

In 1912, Lili and Gerda moved to Paris, where Lili took the name Lili Elbe for herself and began living publicly as a woman, wearing dresses and makeup and growing out her hair. She even accompanied Gerda to public events.

Lili experienced intense gender dysphoria—she wanted to change her body to match her gender identity. She shared her feelings with several doctors, only to be met with confusion or hostility. Can you imagine how isolated she must have felt?

At some point during the 1920s, Lili learned about a series of surgeries with the potential to help her. Dr. Magnus Hirschfeld (1868–1935), who had founded the German Institute for Sexual Science in Berlin in 1919, had pioneered the procedures.

A rally for National Coming Out Day on October 10, 2011

National Coming Out Day is celebrated every year on October 11 in the United States with marches, rallies, and fundraisers. This day was established in 1987 to commemorate the anniversary of the March on Washington for Lesbian and Gay Rights. Similar events are held each March 31, the Transgender Day of Visibility. This day serves to celebrate transgender people.

credit: AUSTEN HUFFORD/Daily (CC BY 2.0)

You can take a tour of the work of Gerda Gottlieb and Lili Elbe at this website. Can you get a sense of their relationship from these paintings?

WARNING: Some of these paintings portray artful nudity.

🔍 AP Lili Elbe

GENDER WONDER

Lili's last name comes from the river that flows through the city of Dresden, Germany, where one of her operations took place.

The surgeries were still experimental in nature, but in 1930, Lili decided to go through with the first of four sex-reassignment operations.

After her second operation, also in 1930, Lili was legally recognized as a woman. She was even issued a new passport with her correct gender and name listed. However, because homosexual marriage was not legal at the time, Lili's marriage to Gerda was ruled null and void. The two parted ways before Lili's third surgery, which took place in 1931.

Soon, Lili became engaged to a French art dealer, Claude Lejeune. Lili wrote that she was eager to find a way to have biological children, saying, "The fervent longing in my woman's life is to become the mother of a child."

Lili Elbe, 1930

credit: Wellcme Collection (CC BY 4.0)

It was due to this desire that Lili decided to undergo a fourth surgery, in June 1931, to have a uterus transplanted into her body. Unfortunately, Lili's surgery took place nearly 50 years before the development of the drug ciclosporin, which prevents the rejection of organs in modern transplant patients. Her body rejected the implanted uterus and she developed a deadly infection on September 13, 1931.[2, 3]

After her death, Lili remained an inspiration to many. She was remembered as a pioneer whose choices paved the way for other transgender people. Lili once summed up her attitude toward her medical transition by writing, "It is not with my brain, not with my eyes, not with my hands that I want to be creative, but with my heart and with my blood."

Lili's biography, titled *Man into Woman*, was published in 1933. In 2000, *The Danish Girl*, a fictionalized novel by David Ebershoff based on Lili's life, was published. In 2015, *The Danish Girl* was made into a movie starring Eddie Redmayne (1982–) as Lili Elbe and Alicia Vikander (1988–) as Gerda Gottlieb. Alicia won an Academy Award for Best Supporting Actress for her role in the film.

CHRISTINE JORGENSEN

Born in New York, Christine Jorgensen was a trans woman who was assigned the gender of male at birth. She later became the second identifiable person to medically transition. As America's first transgender celebrity, she brought great awareness to the American transgender community.

INVISIBILITY INTERSEX

Throughout history, intersex people have struggled to be publicly acknowledged as a distinct group. Gender reassignment surgery is often performed on the genitals of intersex people born with ambiguous genitalia before they are old enough to consent to or even remember the procedures. As a result, many intersex people grow up without knowing the truth about their physical sex. This can cause great distress for intersex people as they grow up, especially if their gender identity does not match the physical sex that they were assigned. Because of this, most intersex-rights organizations and several medical organizations, including the North American Society for Pediatric and Adolescent Gynecology and the American Medical Students Association, recommend against unnecessary genital-normalizing surgery for intersex infants.

Christine spent her childhood in the Belmont neighborhood of the Bronx in New York City. In her autobiography, Christine described her childhood self as a "frail, blond, introverted little boy who ran from fistfights and rough-and-tumble games." Throughout her early life, Christine experienced gender dysphoria. She described the feeling as having been "born in the wrong body" and "lost between the sexes."[4]

Just after Christine's high school graduation in 1945, she was drafted into the U.S. Army at the age of 19. It was during her time in the military that Christine came across an article about Dr. Christian Hamburger (1904–1992), a Danish doctor who was experimenting with hormone therapy in animals. After returning home to America in 1946, Christine continued to read about Dr. Hamburger's work.

In 1950, Christine arranged a trip to Copenhagen on the pretense of visiting family. While there, she made an appointment to speak with Dr. Hamburger. Christine found him to be very helpful and understanding of her situation. She later wrote that although she herself was struggling with her identity, "Dr. Hamburger didn't feel there was anything particularly strange about it."

He diagnosed Christine as transsexual, a term some in the medical community still use today to describe transgender people, and helped Christine begin the process of medically transitioning. Christine underwent hormone therapy and, with encouragement from her doctor, began dressing and living as a woman full-time. Christine was so grateful for Dr. Hamburger's help that she decided to change her first name to Christine in honor of Dr. Hamburger's own first name, Christian.

Although gender reassignment surgery was not outlawed in Denmark, castration, or the removal of the testicles, was. Christine's psychologist, Dr. Georg Stürup (1905–1988), believed that Christine was a good candidate for gender reassignment surgery, and so petitioned the Danish government to allow for castration in Christine's case. With permission granted, in 1950, Christine underwent the first of several surgical procedures. Notes from Lili Elbe's 1930 and 1931 surgeries greatly aided the medical team operating on Christine.

After her operations, Christine was ready to come out to her family and return home. In her autobiography, Christine states that she wrote her mother a letter, saying, "Nature made a mistake which I have had corrected, and now I am your daughter."

> Christine's family was supportive of her transition. However, word of her transformation spread through Denmark and America while she was still recovering in the hospital.

When Christine returned to the United States in 1953, she was met at the airport by reporters. Headlines that would be extremely offensive by today's standards, such as "Surgery Makes Ex-GI Girl" and "Ex-GI Becomes Blonde Beauty," made the front page of several national newspapers.

Overall, however, Christine found the American public to be supportive and mostly respectful. Christine decided to embrace her fame, and began giving interviews for a fee.

You can watch a short documentary about Christine Jorgenson at this website. How do you think the public would treat Christine's story today? Can you think of other people with a similar story?

🔍 Christine Jorgenson video

OFFICIAL FORMS

In the United States, a lot of important paperwork, such as voter registrations, passport applications, and driver's license applications, ask people to select their gender. But usually, only two genders are offered: male or female. For nonbinary people, this poses a big problem. They have to either select an incorrect gender or go without important documents, such as passports or driver's licenses. Because of this, some states and countries have added other gender selections to certain official forms.

Christine took control of her own story by taking advantage of the media attention to educate people about transgender issues and how being transgender is different from being gay.

She discovered a love for singing, dancing, and comedy—these were passions she had always suppressed before her transition. Soon, she developed a nightclub act and began touring the country. She kept the show lighthearted and included the song "I Enjoy Being a Girl" in her act.

In an interview in 1970, Christine told *The New York Times*, "At first I was very self-conscious and very awkward, but once the notoriety hit, it did not take me long to adjust. I decided if they wanted to see me, they would have to pay for it."[5]

Christine Jorgensen, 1954

You can read Christine Jorgensen's obituary in *The New York Times*. Are you surprised at her views on the women's liberation movement?

Jorgensen obit NYT

credit: Maurice Seymour

Christine published her autobiography, *Christine Jorgensen: A Personal Biography*, in 1967. In 1970, a fictionalized movie, *The Christine Jorgensen Story*, based on Christine's book, was made with 10 percent of the royalties going to Christine herself.[7]

> Christine was the first identifiable American to medically transition, and the first internationally famous case of medical transition.

Her life was often spoken of during the different LGBTQ rights movements of the 1960s, 1970s, and 1980s. A few years before her death from cancer in 1989, Christine said of herself and the doctors who helped her, "We didn't start the sexual revolution but I think we gave it a good kick in the pants!"

Early transgender pioneers such as Lili Elbe and Christine Jorgensen made people more aware of gender identity issues and paved the way for transgender and nonbinary people who came out after them. In the next chapter, we'll explore how the transgender movement began in the United States, and the kinds of struggles transgender and nonbinary people had to endure in their quest for equality.

DIFFERENT NARRATIVES

A "narrative" is a particular way of telling, or framing, a story. Two stories might contain similar events, but the language used to describe them can make them very different. Not all transgender people use the same narrative to tell their stories. For example, some transgender people might describe themselves as being or having been "trapped in the wrong body." Other transgender people may feel that their bodies were never wrong, but were simply mislabeled by other people. Some believe that medical transition "turns" a person from one gender to another. Others feel that they were their true gender all along and that medical transition simply helped them look the way they felt. Every person's story is different, and the best expert on any individual's story is that individual.

KEY QUESTIONS

- **What is coming out? Does a person have to tell everyone in their life about their gender identity in order to come out?**

- **What are some issues that intersex people face in trying to come out and be recognized as a distinct group?**

THE STORIES OF LILI ELBE

Several versions of Lili Elbe's life story exist for anyone to read or watch. The first is Lili's 1933 biography, *Man into Woman.* This book was written by German journalist and translator Ernst Harthern (1884–1969) under the pen name of Niels Hoyer, and contains many of Lili's own writings. The second version of Lili's life story is *The Danish Girl,* a fictionalized novel published in 2000.

- **Do some research about the life of Lili Elbe.** Visit a library or go online to read more about her. You can also read the books mentioned in the introduction.

- **What do you notice about different stories of her life?** Do some contain different facts? Do any use her deadname or a male pronoun when describing her? Why do you think this happens? Which sources do you think provide a more accurate depiction of Lili's life? Why?

- **Take notes and create a slideshow, essay, or other creative display of your findings.** Be sure to use credible sources that respect her transgender identity.

- **Present your work to another person who has also done this activity.** Are your conclusions the same? What differences are there?

To investigate more, compare descriptions of Lili Elbe's life with descriptions of the lives of transgender people today. How do they differ? Do you think we use language today that will seem offensive 30 years in the future?

Chapter 2 ▶
The Birth of a Movement

ONE LOUD VOICE LEADS TO MANY!

How did transgender and nonbinary people organize to fight for equal rights?

American culture has become more accepting of transgender and nonbinary people in recent decades. This is largely because of the efforts of the LGBTQ rights movement, which began in the 1960s and is still thriving today.

The 1960s were a time of great cultural change in the United States. Have you ever heard stories about the Vietnam War, the draft, the civil rights movement, or the women's liberation movement? All these began in the 1960s, a time when many people decided that change was needed in the United States to create a fairer and more equal society. People felt that standing up for individual rights was important.

The gay rights movement, now often called the LGBTQ movement, also began during this time. Transgender, nonbinary, gay, and lesbian people, among others, demanded equality.

Like many cultural movements of the time, the gay rights movement involved clashes with law enforcement and other struggles. Several riots occurred in the beginning of the movement. Even peaceful protesters were sometimes arrested, beaten, injured, or even killed. But people also began to recognize that transgender and nonbinary people deserved equal rights.

COMPTON CAFETERIA RIOT

The Compton Cafeteria Riot was an important event that happened at the beginning of the LGBTQ rights movement. To understand why the riot happened, we must examine how different life was for LGBTQ Americans during the 1960s from how it is today.

Cross-dressing means putting on clothing that is associated with a different gender. During the 1960s, cross-dressing was illegal in many places in the United States. Drag performers were often arrested going to or from shows, which affected their ability to earn money to support themselves.

> Transgender women, transgender men, and nonbinary people could be arrested for expressing their gender identity.

Cross-dressing was illegal in San Francisco, California, during the 1960s. But San Francisco also had a thriving LGBTQ community. One popular place for LGBTQ San Franciscans to live, work, and hang out was the Tenderloin neighborhood in downtown San Francisco. It was one of the only places where drag performers and transgender people lived openly. But even in the Tenderloin, police often arrested LGBTQ people.

The Tenderloin was also home to a 24-hour diner called Compton's Cafeteria. The diner became a popular place for LGBTQ San Franciscans to gather and socialize, often late at night. Compton's was an especially important gathering place for transgender people, since even some gay nightclubs barred transgender people from entering.

ERICKSON EDUCATIONAL FOUNDATION

Reed Erickson (1917–1992) was an important transgender activist during the 1960s. Reed came out as a transgender man in 1963 and began the process of medically transitioning. During this time, Reed decided to use his wealth to help other LGBTQ people. In 1964, Reed created the Erickson Educational Foundation. It funded research about transgender people and opened the first North American gender clinic at Johns Hopkins University. It also sponsored educational efforts, such as public addresses, films, pamphlets, and books, and organized some of the earliest international conferences on transgenderism. These conferences eventually became the World Professional Association for Transgender Health, a nonprofit organization that still exists today.

However, Compton Cafeteria's management wasn't always friendly to their LGBTQ customers. Sometimes, management called the police late at night to have LGBTQ people cleared. Police often arrested anyone they considered to be cross-dressing. Because of these frequent police raids, tension grew between LGBTQ San Franciscans and the police force.

Compton's Cafeteria Riot Commemoration 40th Anniversary Historical Marker, San Francisco, California

credit: Gaylesf

TOGETHER WE STAND

The LGBTQ movement consisted of different organizations, headed by different LGBTQ people, fighting for equality in their own ways. Progress has been made along different lines for gay people, lesbian people, transgender people, and nonbinary people, because different LGBTQ groups fought against oppression using a variety of methods. The LGBTQ movement, which is still alive and well today, made Americans more aware of LGBTQ people, including transgender and nonbinary people, and the ways they needed support.

One night in 1966, a police officer at Compton's grabbed a drag queen as he was trying to arrest her and she threw a cup of coffee in the officer's face. According to Amanda St. Jaymes, a transgender woman who was at Compton's that night, the diner erupted into a full-blown riot between police officers and LGBTQ customers.

"We just got tired of it," Amanda said in an interview with historian Susan Stryker (1961–). "We wanted our rights."[1]

The Compton's Cafeteria Riot was one of the first LGBTQ-related riots in recorded history, though many peaceful protests and other demonstrations had come beforehand. The riot didn't get much attention when it happened, but it did help spark a change in the way LGBTQ people interacted with the world around them.

LGBTQ people realized that they didn't have to endure being treated unfairly and inhumanely. Instead, they could stand up for their rights and fight back.

Street art in San Francisco

credit: Gary Stevens (CC BY 2.0)

TANYA WISCHERATH

THE COMPTON'S CAFETERIA RIOT OCCURRED IN AUGUST OF 1966 IN THE TENDERLOIN, IN RESPONSE TO POLICE BRUTALITY AGAINST THE LGBT COMMUNITY. THIS INCIDENT WAS ONE OF THE FIRST TRANSGENDER RIOTS IN U.S. HISTORY, PRECEEDING THE MORE FAMOUS 1969 STONEWALL RIOTS IN NYC.

ALTHOUGH SAN FRANCISCO CONTINUES TO LEAD IN THE STRUGGLE FOR EQUAL RIGHTS FOR THE LGBTQI COMMUNITY, TRANS WOMEN'S CONTRIBUTIONS ARE OFTEN OVERLOOKED.

THIS MURAL IS A DEDICATION TO THE WORK OF A FEW ACTIVISTS AMONG MANY, WHO HAVE TIRELESSLY FOUGHT FOR A MORE JUST, ACCEPTING, AND RIGHTEOUS SAN FRANCISCO.

VIOLE

SEXISM

EXCLUSION

FEAR

The riot led to protests by LGBTQ groups such as Vanguard, the first recorded gay youth organization in the United States. After the riot, more resources for transgender people began to form in San Francisco, including the National Transsexual Counseling Unit. This was the first peer-run support and advocacy organization for transgender people.

THE STONEWALL RIOTS

The Stonewall Riots of 1969 are considered by many to be the beginning of the LGBTQ rights movement. The cultural impact of these riots stretched far beyond New York City, where they took place. In fact, the riots led to many nationwide changes for the American LGBTQ community, including transgender and nonbinary people.

During the 1960s, New York City was home to a large LGBTQ community, but some state laws and city ordinances made life difficult for LGBTQ people. For example, the city had a statute against cross-dressing, which meant that drag queens and transgender people were often arrested when out in public.

Some places wouldn't serve LGBTQ people or customers that the owners suspected of cross-dressing. What might it be like to be refused service at a restaurant or other business because of who you are or what you're wearing?

LGBTQ New Yorkers did have a few important gathering places where they felt safe from discrimination. These restaurants and clubs were welcoming to gays and lesbians, though some did not admit transgender people. One place, called the Stonewall Inn, was located in New York City's Greenwich Village.

Here, the owners welcomed all LGBTQ people. It was also one of the few places in New York that allowed not only LGBTQ customers, but also dancing! Because of this, it became a popular place for LGBTQ New Yorkers to meet and hang out.

However, like most places where LGBTQ people were welcome, the Stonewall Inn was still subject to frequent police raids. During these raids, NYPD officers would often arrest everyone inside the bar, even if they were not breaking any laws.

During a police raid on June 28, 1969, some customers and neighborhood residents stood outside the Stonewall Inn as police grabbed, hit, and arrested people inside. An angry crowd began to form. How dare the police treat them this way?

> They weren't hurting anyone. They weren't breaking any laws. Their rights were being violated.

At one point, a police officer hit a lesbian on the head as he was forcing her into a police vehicle. The woman yelled at the onlookers, urging them to do something. The angry crowd began to throw things at the police, including loose change and rocks. Finally, a full-blown riot erupted between the crowd and police. Some officers barricaded themselves inside the Stonewall Inn, while the crowd outside attempted to burn the building down.

Eventually, the fire department arrived and the crowd dispersed. But the next night, police showed up at the Stonewall Inn again. They were met by a crowd of thousands of angry LGBTQ New Yorkers, who smashed the windows of police vehicles and even tried to free people who had just been arrested by officers.

THE TERMS, THEY ARE A-CHANGIN'

The meanings of certain words often change over time. Words and terms that were acceptable to use in the past are often offensive today. For example, terms such as sex-change, cross-dresser, transvestite, and transsexual were used in the past, but are not commonly used today. These words are usually used only to talk about historical events and people, to honor the terms that people used to refer to themselves by. Some of these words have even changed in meaning. Using correct, contemporary language to refer to people today is important because it shows respect.

Riots broke out again. Protests sparked
by the Stonewall Riots continued
across New York City for weeks.

Before these protests, LGBTQ people had usually kept quiet about who they were because of the threat of discrimination. In public places, many of them tried to keep from being noticed—it was unusual for lesbians or gay men to show how they felt about their partners in public.

But when crowds of thousands began turning up at riots and protests, LGBTQ New Yorkers felt more secure. They began to be more openly affectionate in public, holding hands and kissing, even though they could be arrested for doing so. The media began to talk more openly about the LGBTQ rights movement.

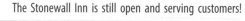

The Stonewall Inn is still open and serving customers!

credit: Eric Fischer (CC BY 2.0)

Cultural changes, including the repeal of some of the most discriminatory laws, began to take place once LGBTQ Americans felt secure enough to protest openly. The Stonewall Riots had a lasting impact on the way that LGBTQ Americans think of themselves, and how the U.S. society thinks of LGBTQ Americans.

Songs, plays, and poems have been written about the riots. Today, the Stonewall Inn itself is classified as a national historic landmark, due to the impact the Stonewall Riots had on the LGBTQ rights movement.

Let's take a look at some of the major figures of the early LGBTQ rights movement. These people were on the frontlines of the revolution. And even as things were improving for people who identified as LGBTQ, the world could still be a dangerous place.

SYLVIA RIVERA

Sylvia Rivera was an LGBTQ, gender non-conforming, Latina activist in the 1960s, 1970s, and 1980s. Her influence led to more inclusion for transgender people in the LGBTQ community during a time when they were often shunned.

> Sylvia usually referred to herself as a "drag queen" or simply as "Sylvia" throughout her life, refusing to put an exact label on her gender identity. Sylvia always referred to herself with she/her pronouns.[2]

Born in New York City, Sylvia Rivera had a difficult childhood. She was assigned the gender of male at birth. Her stepfather was violent and her mother committed suicide when Sylvia was about three years old.

> "I was proud to make the road and help change laws and what-not. I was very proud of doing that and proud of what I'm still doing, no matter what it takes."
>
> —Sylvia Rivera

For a short time, Sylvia lived with her grandmother, who disapproved of Sylvia wearing makeup. By the age of 10, Sylvia was living on her own on the streets of New York. Can you imagine how frightening it must have been to be homeless and alone at such a young age?

As she grew up, Sylvia refused to keep her gender identity a secret. Because of this, she lived with a high risk of violence and discrimination. Eventually, Sylvia was taken in by a group of transgender people, many of whom were homeless. They referred to themselves as "street queens."

> Sylvia believed that transgender people should be included in the LGBTQ rights movement.

Many within the movement disagreed. They argued that straight people would not take the community seriously if it included transgender people. However, Sylvia was a passionate protester and her words helped convince people within the community to change their minds.

Sylvia was present at many LGBTQ protests throughout the 1960s and 1970s. She also marched in defense of women's rights and against the war in Vietnam.

According to Carrie Davis, the chief programs and policy officer at the NYC LGBTQ Community Center, Sylvia Rivera focused on helping the most vulnerable people in the LGBTQ rights movement. "She was one of the first people to highlight that our movement needed to be more inclusive of people who did not fit in the mainstream," Carrie said in an interview with NBC News in 2015. "Sylvia was drawn to helping the poor, the homeless, people of color, gender non-conformists. She used her outsider status to help make change."

In 1970, Sylvia cofounded an organization called STAR (Street Transvestite Action Revolutionaries) with her friend and fellow activist, Marsha P. Johnson. STAR focused on helping young LGBTQ people, especially transgender people, stay off the streets. Sylvia and Marsha also ran a shelter for homeless LGBTQ youth during the early 1970s.

> "STAR was for the street gay people, the street homeless people, and anybody that needed help at that time," Sylvia said, during a 1998 interview for *Workers World*. "Marsha and I just decided it was time to help each other and help other kids. We fed people and clothed people."[3]

Sylvia was also a member of the Gay Liberation Front, which led protests throughout the 1970s. According to Sylvia, her activism was fueled by a desire to see real change. "I was a radical, a revolutionist. I am still a revolutionist."

MARSHA P. JOHNSON

Marsha P. Johnson was an African American LGBTQ activist during the 1960s, 1970s, and 1980s. She participated in the Stonewall Riots and the following year cofounded STAR with her friend and fellow activist, Sylvia Rivera.

Throughout her life, Marsha referred to herself as a "drag queen" and a "transvestite," but those terms have changed in meaning over time. It's impossible to know if Marsha would consider herself a transgender woman, since the term "transgender" was not commonly used during her lifetime. However, we do know that Marsha always referred to herself with she/her pronouns.

THE GLF BANNER

The Gay Liberation Front, or GLF, was an LGBTQ rights organization made up of a collection of gay liberation groups. The first group was formed in 1969, in New York City, shortly after the Stonewall Riots. It was made up of LGBTQ youth who wished to openly protest the injustices facing their generation. They purposefully used the word "gay" in the group's title, even though, at the time, many LGBTQ rights organizations had more cryptic names, such as Mattachine or Jauus. Eventually, the GLF became a collection of many different groups, or "cells." These cells were united under the GLF name, but each had their own unique focus. Throughout the 1960s, many of these cells marched and protested under the GLF banner.

Born in New Jersey in 1945, Marsha was assigned the gender of male at birth. When she began cross-dressing as a child, she was punished by her mother. In a 2012 documentary called *Pay It No Mind—The Life and Times of Marsha P. Johnson*, Marsha said that her mother told her being homosexual was like being "lower than a dog."

Because Marsha could not be herself at home, she decided to leave for New York City after graduating from high school. In 1966, she moved to Greenwich Village.

Marsha eventually began performing as a drag queen. She could not afford to dress in expensive costumes, but she always dressed colorfully and was very charismatic. She grew famous in New York City's LGBTQ community for her warm smile and her willingness to help others. Famously, Marsha said that the "P" in her name stood for "pay it no mind." Any time strangers asked about her gender, Marsha would jokingly tell them, "It stands to pay it no mind."

Marsha was present at the Stonewall Riots on June 28, 1969. In one interview, Marsha said that she arrived around two in the morning, after the riots had started. Once she saw what was happening, she joined in with the crowd, throwing things and chanting words of protest. "We just were saying, no more police brutality and, oh, we had enough of police harassment in the Village and other places," Marsha said.[4]

In 1970, Marsha participated in a sit-in protest at New York University's Weinstein Hall, where the university had cancelled a dance after the university found out that gay organizations were sponsoring the dance. That was the same year Marsha cofounded STAR along with Sylvia Rivera.

GENDER WONDER

The idea that someone could be proud to be LGBTQ, instead of ashamed, gained popularity during the time of the Stonewall Riots. This idea has carried into contemporary times and is especially evident during LGBTQ pride events, such as parades.

A painting of Marsha Johnson and Sylvia Rivera

credit: Gary LeGault

In 1973, Marsha and Sylvia were banned from marching in New York City's gay pride parade because some gay and lesbian New Yorkers did not want to include drag queens. Why do you think they felt this way? Do you think that people who have been on the receiving end of discrimination might be better motivated to include other disenfranchised groups?

It's easy to imagine how hurtful this must have been for Marsha and Sylvia. However, the two of them marched anyway, just ahead of the main parade.

Marsha went on to become a successful drag performer, and even toured the world with several drag performance groups. Marsha P. Johnson remains one of the most important and fondly remembered figures in the LGBTQ rights movement.

In 1992, Marsha's body was found in the Hudson River. Police originally ruled her death a suicide, but many of Marsha's friends believed that she was murdered or that she accidentally fell. The investigation was re-opened in 2017, but no conclusions had been made as of the printing of this book.

> **While legal advances are steps forward, they do bring up the question of who gets to decide what is "normal." How might the world be different if transgender identity were the ruler against which gender was measured, while cisgender identity was considered to be different and unusual?**

• • • • • • • • • • • •

In 2015, the Marsha P. Johnson Institute was established. Its mission is to decrease the amount of violence against transgender people, especially non-white, transgender women, and to build leadership and community among transgender people.[5]

The United States changed greatly during the 1960s. Several civil rights movements, including the LGBTQ rights movement, led to important protests against discrimination during this time. Riots, such as the famous Stonewall Riots, sometimes happened as a result of tensions between citizens and police forces. Civil rights leaders such as Sylvia Rivera and Marsha P. Johnson changed American culture forever by inspiring others to fight for important causes.

LEGAL CHANGES IN THE 1960s AND '70s

In the 1960s, certain federal, state and local laws made life very difficult for LGBTQ people. These ranged from sodomy laws, which banned certain sexual acts between people of the same gender, even in the privacy of their homes, to bans against cross-dressing, which made it nearly impossible for transgender and nonbinary people to express their true gender publicly.

Much of the activism of the 1960s came in direct response to these unjust policies.

Most of these laws did not change until the late 1970s, after the Stonewall Riots and the following years of LGBTQ demonstrations brought national attention to the LGBTQ cause. However, some legal changes took place even before then.

In 1961, Illinois became the first state to repeal its sodomy laws. In 1973, the American Psychiatric Association removed homosexuality from its list of mental disorders, making it legal for gay and lesbian Americans to work in places that had certain mental health requirements for employees.

In 1975, Renée Richards, a transgender woman, was barred from competing in the women's tennis U.S. Open, but in 1977 the Supreme Court of New York overturned the decision, allowing Renée to play. This set a legal precedent that other transgender athletes had a right to compete in their chosen sports.[6]

In the next chapter, we'll explore how the world continued to change for LGBTQ people throughout the late 1960s as well as the 1970s and 1980s.

VOCAB LAB

Write down what you think each word means. What root words can you find to help you? What does the context of the word tell you?

activism, **charismatic**, **civil rights**, **cross-dressing**, **disenfranchised**, **LGBTQ rights movement**, **repeal**, and **riot**.

Compare your definitions with those of your friends or classmates. Did you all come up with the same meanings? Turn to the text and glossary if you need help.

KEY QUESTIONS

- **What are some of the underlying tensions that caused the Compton's Cafeteria Riot? How are they similar to the causes of the Stonewall Riots? How do they differ?**

- **The Compton's Cafeteria Riot and the Stonewall Riots led to many changes for LGBTQ people in the United States. Besides greater legal protections, what were some of these changes?**

TIME TO MOVE!

Now that you know about the beginnings of the LGBTQ rights movement, research the events that sparked one of America's other civil rights movements in the 1960s, such as the African American civil rights movement and the women's liberation movement.

- **What's similar between the beginnings of these two movements?** What's different?

- **Civil rights movements are an important part of the history of the United States.** Can you imagine what life would be like for women if the women's rights movement had never occurred? What about the lives of African Americans—how would they be different if the country had never heard the speeches of Martin Luther King Jr. or seen the power of the March on Washington?

- **Research the early beginnings of a few civil rights movements.** Consider these questions.

  - What did these movements have in common?

  - What was different about them?

  - Did every movement have certain leaders who stood out? What were they like?

  - Did every movement experience clashes with law enforcement? Why?

  - Are there movements just beginning today that have similarities to these movements?

- **Draw a Venn diagram to show what these early movements had in common and how they differed.** What conclusions can you draw from your research?

To investigate more, review your findings with another person who has completed this activity and who chose a different civil rights movement than you did. What can you learn about the similarities and differences between these movements by comparing your research? Did every civil rights movement have something in common?

Chapter 3
Challenges and Changes

THOSE RIGHTS WERE SO WORTH FIGHTING FOR!

AND THEY STILL ARE!

How did early LGBTQ activism affect transgender and nonbinary people around the world?

Early LGBTQ activism led to cultural changes for transgender and nonbinary people. As cultures around the world became more aware of LGBTQ people and the causes they fought for, legal changes began to take place as well.

As LGBTQ activism became more prominent in society, the mainstream media began to openly cover more protests and events. In the United States, the activism that had started in the 1960s began to see some slow outcomes as cities and towns changed the laws to better protect LGBTQ people. Attitudes were changing around the world, too. As the 1970s and '80s saw, transgender people were becoming more visible with each passing protest.

In 1972, Sweden became the first country in the world to allow people to legally change their gender.[1]

This meant that transgender people living in Sweden could medically transition. They could change their birth names on legal documents, such as driver's licenses and birth certificates.

Photo IDs, such as driver's licenses and passports, need to have an accurate picture of what you look like. Can you imagine why someone wouldn't want to use an accurate picture of themselves expressing their female gender identity if their license lists "male" as their gender? For this person, it is important to have their name, photo, and listed gender match in order to avoid confusion and invasive questions.

In 1980, Germany instituted a law that made it possible for people to legally change their first name and gender on official documents. However, a person could do this only after having sex reassignment surgery.

> Sex reassignment surgery is the surgical portion of medical transition. A common misconception is that people have just one sex reassignment surgery, but people can choose to have many kinds of surgeries when they medically transition.

Not everybody wants to have the same kind of surgery. This is especially since certain sex reassignment surgeries can cause sterility, or the inability to have children.

In fact, Germany's law required that transgender people be sterilized before they could change their name and gender on official documents. So, while this law helped some transgender people, it was also very harmful. Why should the right to have children be taken away in order for someone to be able to change their legal documents? In 2011, Germany's Supreme Court ruled that the sterilization requirement was unconstitutional and overturned it.

MATCH UP

Why is it so important for people to be able to change their legal documents? Just think of all the things that require you to have accurate identification! Driving, traveling to other countries, getting insurance, and buying a home would be much more complicated if your identifying papers didn't match the name and gender you use to fill out paperwork.

GENDER WONDER

Beginning in the 1970s, some countries implemented laws recognizing genders in addition to male and female, and some made it legal to medically transition from one gender to another.

MISUNDERSTANDING MEDICAL TRANSITION

There are many misunderstandings about what it means to medically transition. These misunderstandings can lead to attitudes and even laws that are harmful, so it is important to understand what medical transition is and how it helps transgender people.

The most common misunderstanding is that there is only one sex reassignment surgery, and that a transgender person hasn't truly transitioned until they have had this one surgery. Because of this idea, some countries and even some states in the United States require transgender people to have surgery in order to legally change their names and genders on legal documents.

In reality, many different surgical sex reassignment procedures are available. These include procedures to remove breast tissue or apply breast implants, surgery that changes a person's genitals, and procedures that alter a person's facial features, voice, and more.

> Not every transgender person wants or needs all these procedures. Some transgender people choose not to have any surgeries.

Hormone therapy is another important part of medical transition for many transgender people. Some people choose to do just hormone therapy, without any surgery.

A transgender person is always the gender they say they are. It doesn't matter how they publicly dress, how they look, or how they sound. It doesn't matter whether a transgender person has undergone surgical procedures, hormone treatment, or no medical treatment at all—they are still the gender they claim.

Remember, gender identity is separate from physical sex. A person doesn't need to change their body in order to have a gender identity that is different from the one they were assigned at birth.

It is also important to remember that medical procedures are a personal, private choice, whether a person is cisgender, nonbinary, or transgender. This is especially true when it comes to sex reassignment surgeries and hormone therapy, since some of these procedures involve private parts of the body. Nobody wants a stranger to ask about the kinds of medicines you take or the kinds of surgeries you've had!

Let's meet a few of the people who continued to champion the rights of LGBTQ people during the second half of the twentieth century, when countries around the world continued to make gradual progress toward granting equal rights to all.

SIR LADY JAVA

Born in New Orleans, Louisiana, in 1943, Sir Lady Java is an African-American, transgender woman. She sang, performed comedy, and became a transgender activist during the late 1960s and throughout the 1970s.

This magazine clipping shows Sir Lady Java protesting Los Angeles's ordinance against cross-dressing.

presstelegram
Sir Lady Java

Assigned the gender of male at birth, she had a supportive mother who helped her transition at an early age. Performing at local clubs in New Orleans, long known as a place that was accepting of people and ideas that were different, Sir Lady Java gained popularity with her comedic talent.

In her early twenties, Sir Lady Java moved to Los Angeles, California, where her performances quickly became well-known in night clubs around the city. It was in Los Angeles that Sir Lady Java became famous for helping overturn a city-wide ordinance banning cross-dressing.

In 1967, the Los Angeles Police Department began shutting down venues where Sir Lady Java performed. At the time, a city ordinance known locally as "Rule Number 9" made it illegal to cross-dress in Los Angeles. Sir Lady Java protested, picketing outside the well-known Redd Foxx Club despite being told to stay away.

When a reporter asked why she felt it was so important to protest, she answered, "It's got to stop somewhere, and it won't unless somebody steps forward and takes a stand. I guess that's me."

Sir Lady Java hired a lawyer from the American Civil Liberties Union (ACLU) and challenged Rule Number 9 in court. This made her the first transgender performer the ACLU ever backed. Her lawyer argued that the city ordinance infringed upon Sir Lady Java's rights by taking away her main source of income. The courts rejected her legal challenge, but because of the attention that Sir Lady Java had brought to the rule, it was challenged again, and in 1969, it was finally struck down.

Following her legal battle, Sir Lady Java became even more well known. She was profiled in *JET Magazine* and featured in local newspapers. She continued to perform throughout the 1970s while speaking out against discriminatory laws that targeted transgender people.

Sir Lady Java's activism was especially important for other African American transgender people, who had even fewer civil rights and faced even more violence than white transgender people. In June 2016, Sir Lady Java was a guest of honor at the 18th annual Trans Pride L.A. Festival.

A marcher holding a sign with the names of iconic transgender people, including Sir Lady Java

credit: Alec Perkins (CC BY 2.0)

LEE GREER BREWSTER

Lee Greer Brewster (1943–2000) was an activist and writer who fought for civil rights for transgender people, nonbinary people, cross-dressers, and drag performers throughout the 1970s.[5] He was the first well-known business owner whose business offered services specifically for cross-dressers. Lee used he/him pronouns and described himself as a cross-dresser or transvestite.

During the late 1950s and early 1960s, Lee worked for the U.S. Federal Bureau of Investigation (FBI). However, the FBI fired him when officials discovered he was gay. Soon after, Lee moved to New York City, where he began performing as a drag queen.

He became active in a gay rights organization called the Mattachine Society and began hosting fundraisers as well as elaborate parties, called balls, for the organization at a nearby hotel. These balls eventually became extremely popular in the New York LGBTQ scene, especially during the 1970s. Guests would dress in elaborate costumes and outfits to attend.

> Today, the drag community still fondly remembers this "ballroom culture" that Lee made famous.

Lee eventually opened Lee's Mardi Gras Boutique, which sold clothing specifically for cross-dressing men. The business was a success, although Lee was careful to keep the store's location private—that way, only people in the LGBTQ community could find it. Lee wanted to protect his customers from harassment.

HISTORICAL DISCRIMINATION

During the 1960s, 1970s and 1980s, many state and federal laws made life difficult for LGBTQ people. Some laws made cross-dressing and even homosexual relationships illegal. Laws called "sodomy laws" outlawed certain sexual acts between LGBTQ people, even in the privacy of their own homes. In addition to state and federal laws, ordinances and other rules made life harder for LGBTQ people in some cities.

In 1969, Lee founded the Queens Liberation Front, a civil rights organization for cross-dressers and people he described as transvestites. Throughout the 1970s, Lee participated in public marches and protests on behalf of the LGBTQ community. He also wrote and published *Drag Magazine*—a publication specifically for drag performers and cross-dressers.

In the early 1970s, Lee convinced the New York City Department of Consumer Affairs to remove homosexuals from a list of people who could lawfully be removed from public spaces at any time. Lee felt that the rule gave police an excuse to harass and intimidate LGBTQ New Yorkers.

People such as Lee and Sir Lady Java worked tirelessly to advance the rights of LGBTQ people through protests, performances, the media, and any legal avenue they could find. Because of them, life gradually got better for transgender people.

> The greater community began to accept that people could be different, and discriminatory laws and rules were challenged.

INTERNAL DIVISION

During the 1970s and 1980s, the LGBTQ community in the United States was changing, along with the rest of American culture. Some gay and lesbian people, however, still did not want to associate with transgender people, nonbinary people, or others they considered to be cross-dressers, concerned they made it more difficult for the LGBTQ community to be accepted and understood by those on the outside.

SUCCESS IN CHICAGO

In 1851, Chicago, Illinois, passed a city ordinance making it a criminal offense for anyone to appear in public "in a dress not belonging to his or her sex."[6] The ordinance was overturned in 1973, mainly because the LGBTQ rights movement had made a point to campaign against the ordinance and educate voters about how it harmed their community.

Some feminists felt that transgender women were a threat to feminism. They felt that transgender women were not really women, but were actually men trying to invade women-only spaces. This was a huge concern for some people, as the feminist movement was making its own strides forward throughout the 1960s, 1970s, and 1980s. As women gained more social, political, and personal power, feminists feared these advances might be threatened by transgender people.

In 1973, a lesbian organization called the West Coast Lesbian Conference held a vote about whether to allow transgender folk singer Beth Elliott (1950–) to perform at an event they were hosting. The vote allowed Beth to perform, but it was very close— many members opposed her performance.

Beth left right after her performance to avoid confrontation with angry members. That same year, the San Francisco chapter of the Daughters of Bilitis, the first lesbian political and civil rights group in the United States, kicked Beth out.[7]

EVEN WITHIN QUEER COMMUNITIES, THERE'S STILL A LOT OF DISCRIMINATION!

REALLY?! GROSS!

YEAH! QUEER CISGENDER FOLKS CAN BE REALLY NASTY TO TRANS AND NONBINARY FOLKS.

WE ALL NEED TO SUPPORT EACH OTHER, ALWAYS!

EVERYONE'S IDENTITIES ARE VALID!

Beth had served as the group's vice president and had edited the chapter's newsletter, called *Sisters*, which explored issues facing the lesbian community in San Francisco. But despite the work she had done, the Daughters of Bilitis expelled Beth because of her gender identity. Why did transgender woman inspire such vitriol?

> The members who voted to expel Beth equated physical sex with gender identity and did not believe that they could be different.

Today, divisions still exist in the LGBTQ community. Some people, who call themselves Trans Exclusionary Radical Feminists (TERFs), still insist that transgender women should not have a place in women's spaces, such as women's restrooms or organizations meant only for women. Others still feel that drag performers and openly transgender people hurt the image of the overarching LGBTQ community. What might this mean for LGBTQ rights?

THE AIDS CRISIS

HIV (human immunodeficiency virus) is a virus that attacks the body's immune system. As time passes, untreated HIV destroys a person's ability to fight off even minor infections. It leads to AIDS (acquired immunodeficiency syndrome), the most severe stage of HIV infection.[8]

Today, people with HIV can live long, healthy lives thanks to modern medicine, and some people with HIV never develop AIDS. Because HIV is spread only through blood, certain sexual contact, childbirth, and breast milk, its spread is preventable.

SUCCESS IN MINNEAPOLIS

In 1975, Minneapolis, Minnesota, became the first city in the United States to pass an ordinance protecting transgender people against discrimination. The law stated that no one could be discriminated against on the basis of "having or projecting a self-image not associated with one's biological maleness or one's biological femaleness."[9]

Because of ignorance
surrounding HIV and AIDS
and the already-present
prejudice against the
LGBTQ community, the
American public reacted
poorly to the epidemic.

However, no one knew this in the mid-to-late 1970s, when Americans began dying of a mysterious illness. Most patients were gay men and transgender women, leading people to call the disease gay-related immune deficiency (GRID). It wasn't until 1982 that the Centers for Disease Control realized that the illness wasn't isolated to the LGBTQ community, and the term "AIDS" was introduced. HIV was not yet known as the cause of AIDS, and little was known about its spread. The 1980s faced what has come to be known as the AIDS epidemic, or AIDS crisis.

Though many non-LGBTQ people had developed the disease, it was mostly thought of as an LGBTQ illness. This led to further discrimination against LGBTQ people and anyone living with HIV or AIDS. False information, such as the idea that the disease could be spread by hugging or holding someone's hand, was unfortunately believed by many.

In 1984, a 13-year-old boy named Ryan White was diagnosed with HIV. He was barred from attending middle school in Kokomo, Indiana, for fear that his infection would spread to other students. Ryan's family fought a legal battle that ultimately allowed him to return to school, but he faced harassment and threats when he came back.[10]

Ronald Reagan was president of the United States during the majority of the AIDS Crisis. His administration has been criticized for its unwillingness to recognize the crisis. Reagan did not address the crisis in-depth until 1987, after almost 23,000 Americans had died.[11]

Rates of HIV and AIDS have fallen dramatically since the 1980s. Today, people with HIV can lead long, normal lives thanks to greater knowledge and medical advancements.

A CHANGE IN SPORTS HISTORY

Sometimes, an individual's struggle for equal rights becomes a very public symbol. Renée Richards (1934–) is a transgender woman. She was a professional tennis player who fought for the right to participate in the U.S. Tennis Open in 1977.[12] Her decision to compete in women's tennis opened doors for transgender athletes who came after her.

Assigned the gender of male at birth, Renée Richards was athletic throughout her childhood, playing many different sports. Renée realized that she was transgender at an early age but kept it to herself, since being transgender was considered a mental illness at the time. During her teenage years, Renée read the book *Man into Woman*, about the life of Lili Elbe, the first person known to medically transition. Renée desperately wanted to transition herself, but kept that desire bottled up, using sports as an outlet for her frustration.

> During college, Renée began dressing in female clothes in private.

She began calling herself Renée, which means "reborn" in French. After graduating from Yale University, Renée did the best she could to live what she considered a normal life. She became a doctor, joined the Navy, played competitive men's tennis, and started a family. But her desire to medically transition never went away.

She intended to travel to North Africa and see Dr. Georges Burou (1910–1987), a surgeon who performed sex reassignment surgeries. But Renée was too afraid to go through with her plan, and continued to live publicly as a man.

Renée said that sports helped her through the hardest parts of her young life. "During this period, I probably would not have survived without tennis. Athletics was the one constant in an otherwise uncertain world," she said.

Finally, in the early 1970s, Renée realized that she could not hide her gender identity any longer. She decided to medically transition, undergoing surgery in 1975, at the age of 40, and legally changing her gender. After her transition, Renée moved across the country to California, and began practicing as a doctor in Newport Beach. Soon, she began playing women's tennis under her new name.

However, Renée's iconic left-hand serve meant she was recognized during a competition. The media reported that she was a man in women's clothing, which forced Renée to set the record straight and explain that she was transgender. After her announcement, some athletes refused to play against Renée and boycotted competitions where she appeared. The U.S. Tennis Association (USTA) began making all players take chromosome tests in order to play.

Renée refused to take the test, and was denied entry into the 1976 U.S. Open, the largest tennis competition in the country. Renée was devastated, and eventually decided to sue for her right to play, arguing that she was legally recognized as a woman and should be allowed to compete. In one interview, Renée said that she decided to fight for her rights to "prove that transsexuals as well as other persons fighting social stigmas can hold their heads up high."

Eventually, Renée won her case and was allowed to compete in the 1977 U.S. Open. While she lost her singles match in the first round of the tournament, she went on to the finals in doubles.

After a successful women's tennis career, Renée retired at the age of 47. She went on to become a women's tennis coach, coaching famous tennis player Martina Navratilova (1956–).

Watch this short clip of Renée Richards in 2011 at the Jacob Burns Film Festival speaking about her experiences. Why do you think transgender sports figures might have additional challenges?

Renée Richards at the JBFC

Renée's decision to fight for her rights opened doors for other transgender athletes. It set a legal precedent, or standard, that transgender people should not be discriminated against in athletic competition.

Around the world, transgender and nonbinary people grew more visible throughout the 1970s and 1980s. Countries such as Sweden and Germany began to recognize the existence of transgender people for the first time. Cities in the United States, such as Chicago and Minneapolis, repealed local laws that discriminated against transgender and nonbinary people.

Activists such as Lou Sullivan educated their communities about the issues faced by transgender and nonbinary people, while celebrities such as Renée Richards made more Americans aware that anyone could be transgender or nonbinary.

In the next chapter, we'll learn how transgender and nonbinary people increased their political presence in the 1990s, and how the American media began to cover violence against them more widely.

VOCAB LAB

Write down what you think each word means. What root words can you find to help you? What does the context of the word tell you?

boycott, **medically transition**, **misconception**, **picket**, **precedent**, **sterility**, and **stigma**.

Compare your definitions with those of your friends or classmates. Did you all come up with the same meanings? Turn to the text and glossary if you need help.

KEY QUESTIONS

- Why might a town develop an ordinance that discriminates against transgender people? What emotions might be driving the townspeople?
- Why did some members of the feminist movement object to the inclusion of transgender women? Do you think that made feminists' efforts weaker or stronger?

AROUND THE WORLD

Within the United States, laws that dictate the rights and protections of the LGBTQ community can vary state by state and even by town. Other countries have their own sets of laws. How might these laws reflect the values and attitudes of a nation? What do they say about a country? Find out by doing some research at the library or on the internet.

- **Choose five countries at random.** Exclude the country where you currently live.

- **Research the kinds of laws against and protections for transgender people that exist in these countries, if any.** Are there laws against homosexuality, cross-dressing, or being transgender? If yes, what are the penalties for breaking such laws? Are there any laws that govern other groups of people?

- **Where on the globe are your countries located?** Do you notice any patterns in the laws according to the location of a country? Does any continent host countries with stricter laws governing LGBTQ people?

> **To investigate more,** compare these with someone who chose different countries than you. What new information can you learn about the country or countries you did not choose? Do most of the countries you and your partners chose have protections for transgender people or laws against them? Why do you think this is?

Chapter 4
Violence and Progress in the 1990s

SOMETIMES, JUST BEING YOURSELF CAN SURE BE DANGEROUS.

How did the world become aware of the violence inflicted on the transgender community?

During the 1990s, the media began to focus more on the disproportionate amount of violence inflicted upon transgender and nonbinary people. This made the general public more aware of the dangers that transgender and nonbinary people faced, and inspired some legal and cultural changes around the world.

The 1990s were a time of great change for LGBTQ people around the world. During this decade, several countries passed laws that protected transgender and nonbinary people from discrimination or allowed them to legally change their gender for the first time.

The 1990s were also a time when violence against transgender and nonbinary people became better known to the general public. This was because of increased media coverage of the issues that LGBTQ people faced around the world.

INCREASED VISIBILITY

In 1992, the first International Conference on Transgender Law and Employment Policy took place in Houston, Texas. The conference was organized by Phyllis Frye (ca. 1946–), a transgender woman who was an activist and practicing lawyer in Houston. She had played an important role in repealing Houston's law against cross-dressing 10 years earlier.

The purpose of the conference was to bring attention to the legal issues faced by transgender people. The hope was to develop strategies for changing laws that discriminated against them. Speakers included local judges and others within the Houston law community. The conference eventually added workshops on topics such as education on transgender issues, imprisonment law, and the international bill of gender rights.

Visibility is important for minority communities because it helps the public to be more aware of them and the issues they face. However, visibility does not always increase tolerance. In fact, as coverage of the transgender and nonbinary communities has increased, so has the violence against them, even as they continue to gain more legal rights and equalities.

> Some describe visibility as a double-edged sword, because it is difficult to fight for civil rights without visibility, but it can also make minority communities targets for more violence.

In 1993, Minnesota became the first state in America to list transgender people as a protected class. The state amended the existing Minnesota Human Rights Act to protect transgender people from discrimination in employment, housing, and more. This breakthrough was only possible because of the increased visibility of the transgender community, brought about by the LGBTQ rights movement and events such as the International Conference on Transgender Law and Employment Policy.

INTERNATIONAL CHANGES

In 1992, the European Court of Human Rights ruled that transgender people must be able to legally change their gender on official documents. In 1993, Switzerland passed a law allowing transgender people to apply to have their gender legally changed. In 1999, the United Kingdom extended its existing Sex Discrimination Act to include transgender people, making it illegal to discriminate against them in the areas of employment and vocational training.

In 2010, Phyllis Frye became the first openly transgender judge in the United States.

POLITICAL PRESENCE

The LGBTQ rights movement is much more than just marches, protests, and meetings. A lot of work goes into gaining political power as well. Politics are where new laws are developed, old laws are repealed, and power can be dispersed more equally.

The political influence of the American LGBTQ community grew significantly in the 1990s. In 1995, the first national political organization devoted to issues of gender identity and expression was created in Washington, DC. It was called the Gender Public Advocacy Coalition, or GenderPAC.

GenderPAC was established by Phyllis Frye, the same transgender activist who organized the International Conference on Transgender Law and Employment Policy, and Riki Anne Wilchins (1952–), a transgender activist and author. In 1996, GenderPAC organized its first National Gender Lobby Day. On this day, activists from GenderPAC met with members of the U.S. Congress to discuss discrimination and violence against transgender and nonbinary people.

Watch this video of Riki Anne Wilchins accepting an award for Activist of the Year from Emerging Practitioners in Philanthropy, as she discusses activism, intersectionality, and the work she still wants to see done in the future.

EPIP Riki Wilchins

ONCE WE GOT OUR FOOT IN THE DOOR POLITICALLY, LOTS OF THINGS CHANGED.

POLITICS AFFECTS EVERYONE!

AND REACHES EVERYONE!

YOU CAN FOLLOW LOCAL POLITICS, TOO, EVEN IF YOU CAN'T VOTE YET!

- WHO'S YOUR MAYOR?
- WHAT'S THEIR STANCE ON GENDER ISSUES?

GenderPAC developed a Congressional Diversity Pledge, which they asked members of Congress to sign. The pledge stated that the signer would not discriminate against their own employees based on gender identity or expression. Eventually, almost 200 members of Congress signed the pledge.

To help bring attention to the disproportionate amount of violence transgender people faced in the United States, GenderPAC produced a research project in 1997 called *The First National Study on Transviolence*. It detailed the number of violent crimes reported by transgender people across the country. In 1999, GenderPAC became a member of the Hate Crimes Coalition, a group dedicated to passing hate crime laws in the United States.

Hate crime laws usually state that anyone who commits a hate crime—a crime motivated by hatred for a certain race, religion, sexual orientation, or gender identity—will face harsher punishment than they would for committing a similar crime not motivated by hatred.

GenderPAC's research on transgender violence was referenced during debate over a new hate crime law, called the Matthew Shepard and James Byrd Jr. Hate Crimes Prevention Act. The law was passed in 2009. GenderPAC went on to host the first National Conference on Gender in 2001, and *Time* magazine named GenderPAC cofounder Riki Anne Wilchins one of 100 national innovators that same year.

GenderPAC focused on creating a safer country for transgender and nonbinary people in the United States by taking political and legal action.

MURDER

In Nebraska in 1993, a 21-year-old transgender man named Brandon Teena was murdered by two former friends who had grown violent and raped Brandon when they discovered that he was transgender. They then killed him a week later. The case drew national attention and sparked important conversations about legal protections for transgender people. It also highlighted the mistreatment that many transgender people face when dealing with the police—Brandon was asked inappropriate questions about his gender identity when he reported the rape. In 1998, the story of Brandon's murder was made into a documentary titled *The Brandon Teena Story*, and later into a movie called *Boys Don't Cry*.

YOU'VE GOT ... SUPPORT!

In the early 1990s, the internet was still new. America Online (AOL) was the primary service provider for internet access. Chatrooms were an important part of AOL, providing a place where specific groups, such as gardeners, car enthusiasts, or sports fans, could meet and discuss their passions. In 1994, Gwendolyn Ann Smith (1967–), a transgender activist famous for starting the national Transgender Day of Remembrance, created a chatroom called the Gazebo.

For the first time, transgender people from around the world could reach other people like themselves. They could openly discuss their lives and the issues they faced without risking physical violence. The Gazebo was especially important for transgender people from rural areas or countries where being transgender was criminalized. For them, the Gazebo offered a supportive community they did not have in the physical world.

A TEACHING TRAILBLAZER

Even as violence against transgender people continued, some events showed that things were improving. Karen Kopriva was an English and drama teacher at Lake Forest High School in Illinois. She came out publicly as a transgender woman in June 1998. This made her the first transgender teacher to come out and transition on the job.

When Karen first came out to school administrators, she realized she might be fired because of her gender identity, even though she had been teaching for more than 15 years. Instead, the administration was mostly supportive and agreed that she should keep her job. However, fearing a backlash from parents, the school decided to release a letter to all parents of students at Lake Forest High School, informing them of Karen's diagnosis of "gender identity disorder" and her transition.

At the time, gender identity disorder was the accepted term for what we now call gender dysphoria. Gender identity disorder was still categorized as a mental illness in 1998.

> Remember, words matter. It's easy to imagine that having such personal information released to a large group of people could be humiliating.

Karen gave permission for the school to send the letter. She wanted it sent during the summer so that her students would not be shocked by her transition when they came back to school in the fall. The letter also stated that school administrators did not believe that Karen's transition would cause any disruptions at school.

Karen's students were widely supportive of her, although the principal of Lake Forest High School would not allow a student reporter to release a story about Karen's transition in the school newspaper. Despite Karen's transition becoming national news, the school year went on normally at Lake Forest High School, and media attention died down.

Karen retired in 2016 after 33 years of teaching. Since leaving the classroom, she has become an activist and public speaker, educating others about gender identity and talking about her unique relationship with her son, who is also transgender.

In a 2018 interview with the *Daily Journal*, Karen said that it's important for people to realize that transgender people are everywhere, and that they are worthy of respect, no matter what they do for a living. "We're people, too, and we are in all walks of life," Karen said. "I was a teacher, but there are dentists, truck drivers. There's everything. In every walk of life, you're going to find transgender people there. The fact that they might not be open about it is about society's acceptance of transgender people, not about anything else."[1]

TRAGIC ORIGINS OF CHANGE

On November 28, 1998, a 34-year-old African American transgender woman named Rita Hester was stabbed to death at her apartment in Allston, Massachusetts, a neighborhood of Boston. Rita had been a well-known member of the Boston LGBTQ community. She was a dancer, musician, and drag performer, and was beloved by many throughout Boston. At Rita's vigil, the Rev. Irene Monroe said, "*Everybody* knew her, especially in the trans community and in the African American LGBTQ communities."[1]

GENDER WONDER

By the time the 1990s ended, it was no longer unheard of for gay people to star in television shows, for musicians to come out as gay and lesbian, and for transgender people to be portrayed on screens large and small.

Rita's murder caused an outpouring of anger and grief in the Boston LGBTQ community. A large candlelight vigil was held for Rita on December 4. The Boston LGBTQ community noticed that *The Boston Globe* and other newspapers used disrespectful language when covering Rita's death. *The Boston Globe* had referred to Rita as "a man who sported long braids and preferred women's clothes."

How might other members of the transgender community have felt? How does this language underscore the disrespect LGBTQ people have had to deal with for decades?

Shortly after Rita's death, Gwendolyn Ann Smith, the same transgender activist who started the AOL Gazebo chatroom in 1994, held a virtual vigil in Rita's memory. Many people showed up online to share their grief over Rita's death and the deaths of all transgender people who had been murdered for expressing their gender identity. Gwendolyn then created the Remembering Our Dead project to chronicle violent crimes committed against transgender people.

In 1999, Gwendolyn organized the first Transgender Day of Remembrance.

Held in November, the month that Rita was killed, the first Transgender Day of Remembrance took place in Boston and other cities across the United States. Members of the LGBTQ community and their allies gathered to mourn the lives of transgender people who had been murdered. These gatherings shed an even larger spotlight on the violence faced by transgender people.

Nancy Nangeroni, the activist who had demanded more respectful media coverage of Rita's murder, said in one interview that she didn't realize how much change would be sparked when Rita was killed. "We knew that we were doing important work, and we knew that we were going to keep doing it until we succeeded. We didn't know that this particular moment would live on as it has, and there are many other stories that need to be told that happened back then," she said.[3]

The Transgender Day of Remembrance is still held each November in cities around the world. The day usually includes a candlelight vigil, speeches, marches, and other activities, such as food drives, to help local transgender communities.

Unfortunately, violence against transgender people still persists around the world.

In 2017, 29 transgender Americans were murdered, making it one of the deadliest years on record for transgender people in the United States. These murders are the direct result of discrimination against transgender people.

Discrimination often leads to feelings of fear, anxiety, and hopelessness for transgender people. Rates of depression and anxiety are high in the transgender community. Suicide rates are also much higher for transgender people than cisgender people. As of 2015, around 41 percent of transgender people attempt suicide because of the discrimination they face in everyday life. Transgender activists around the world continue to fight for visibility, acceptance, and legal protections, which may help shield transgender people from violence.[4]

DAY OF REMEMBRANCE

The Transgender Day of Remembrance, held every year on November 20, was started in 1999 by activist Gwendolyn Ann Smith. It is a day meant to honor the memories of transgender people who have lost their lives to anti-transgender violence. Gwendolyn once said of the event, "The Transgender Day of Remembrance seeks to highlight the losses we face due to anti-transgender bigotry and violence. I am no stranger to the need to fight for our rights, and the right to simply exist is first and foremost."

A FLAG TO FLY

Flags are important symbols. They provide an image for people who belong to certain groups to rally around. They also stand as physical symbols of abstract concepts. Abstract concepts are important ideas that you cannot easily see or touch. For example, many religions have symbols that represent their followers' faith, such as the crucifix in Christianity or the Star of David in Judaism.

Countries have flags to help their citizens feel unified and to evoke a certain idea or emotion in the people who live in that country. For example, what do you feel when you see the flag of your country? What does it represent to you?

> You have probably seen a rainbow-colored flag, known as the "pride flag," "gay pride flag," or "rainbow flag." This flag represents the entire LGBTQ community.

What about the transgender pride flag? This flag is an important symbol for transgender and nonbinary people, who are often not as visible as gay, lesbian, or bisexual people in mainstream culture. The transgender pride flag, which features two blue stripes, two pink stripes and one white stripe in the center, was created in 1999 by a transgender activist named Monica Helms (1951–).

Monica created the transgender pride flag after meeting with Michael Page, a fellow activist who created the bisexual pride flag. She wanted the transgender pride flag to be a symbol of unity for transgender and nonbinary people.

VETERAN ACTIVIST

Monica Helms is a transgender woman. She is also an author and a veteran of the U.S. Navy. In 1996, she joined her hometown's chapter of the U.S. Submarine Veterans (USVI). After Monica transitioned in 1997, she re-applied for membership with the group, but at first USVI told her she could not join. Eventually, USVI allowed her to join, making her the first woman to ever be part of that group.

According to Monica, the flag's stripes represent different gender identities. "The stripes at the top and bottom are light blue, the traditional color for baby boys," she said. "The stripes next to them are pink, the traditional color for baby girls. The stripe in the middle is white, for those who are intersex, transitioning, or consider themselves having a neutral or undefined gender. The pattern is such that no matter which way you fly it, it is always correct, signifying us finding correctness in our lives."[5]

The Transgender Pride Flag was flown for the first time in 2002, at a pride parade in Phoenix, Arizona.

In 2003, Monica Helms founded the Transgender American Veterans Association. She speaks at many LGBTQ pride events and has organized marches for transgender and nonbinary veterans. She has also produced a series of YouTube videos about transgender veterans throughout history.

The Transgender Pride Flag

In an interview with *The Huffington Post*, Monica said that she is most proud to represent transgender veterans. "I'm very proud of being a submariner. The submariners that I met over the years, they're okay with the fact that I served and that I'm now a trans woman. I did the same job they did, and even though I've changed in this way, all of them have changed as well. So, we're all shipmates, as it were. There's a lot of strength in submariners and in their camaraderie."[6]

Progress continued for transgender and nonbinary people throughout the 1990s. Countries such as Switzerland and the United Kingdom passed laws granting more rights to transgender people. Transgender and nonbinary people were increasing their political presence by openly running for elected office and forming legal organizations focused on transgender and nonbinary issues.

At the same time, violence against transgender people, which had always been a problem, was reported more often and occasionally turned into high-profile, famous cases, such as the murder of Brandon Teena. In the next chapter, we'll learn how new technology, especially the internet, gave transgender and nonbinary people new ways to continue their fight for equal rights.

VOCAB LAB 📖

Write down what you think each word means. What root words can you find to help you? What does the context of the word tell you?

amend, **bigotry**, **disproportionate**, **hate crime**, **innovator**, **minority**, **tolerance**, and **visibility**.

Compare your definitions with those of your friends or classmates. Did you all come up with the same meanings? Turn to the text and glossary if you need help.

KEY QUESTIONS

- **What are some ways in which transgender activists sparked change for transgender people in the United States?**
- **What do activists, and anyone living openly as transgender, risk that other people do not? Is this fair?**
- **How can cisgender people be allies to the LGBTQ community?**

ORDER IN THE COURT

Many important legal battles were fought by transgender people during the 1990s. Changing discriminatory laws is a crucial part of gaining equal rights for transgender people. What do those lawsuits consist of? Who is willing to endure the inconvenience and even danger of making a legal claim? Let's find out.

- **Research at least two court cases dealing with transgender rights during the 1990s.** These could be discrimination lawsuits filed by transgender individuals or higher court cases where a legal ruling was at stake.

  - Who were the accusers and defendants?

  - What were their stories?

  - What kinds of arguments were made during these cases?

  - What were the ultimate results of these cases?

- **Note what you learned and present your findings to a group of your peers.** What are their opinions on the arguments made in the cases and their ultimate outcomes?

> **To investigate more,** hold a mock trial based on one of the cases you researched. Each person in your group takes on the role of lawyer, defendant, or plaintiff and argues the case. Are the results different in your group than they were in real life? What might influence the outcome of a trial that involves a transgender person?

Chapter 5
A New Century of Connection

How did the technology of the early twenty-first century change the lives of LGBTQ people?

During the first decade of the twenty-first century, technology was changing rapidly. For the first time, LGBTQ people could reach out to one another via the internet, form supportive online communities, and participate in online activism no matter where they were physically living.

Imagine a young transgender person living in an area without an active LGBTQ community. The communications technology of the early 2000s could allow this person to find websites, chat rooms, and message boards specifically built for transgender people just like themselves. For the first time, this person could hear the stories of other transgender people, come out to people without risking physical danger, and make friends with others who shared similar experiences.

They could be part of a supportive community, no matter where they physically lived. Why might this have been such an important emotional opportunity for LGBTQ individuals?

By the year 2000, the internet was a part of many people's daily lives. Chat rooms and message boards became a way for people to reach out to one another, regardless of where they physically lived. Today, holding a text or video conversation with someone across the globe is common, but early in the twenty-first century, this was still a novelty.

The internet also provided LGBTQ people a new and convenient way to organize politically, and for transgender and nonbinary people to carve out their own specific niche within the larger LGBTQ community. Blogs, websites, and online communities dedicated to and run by transgender and nonbinary people meant these groups could find and connect with each other for emotional, practical, and political support. The internet's popularity also gave LGBTQ people a powerful new way to gain visibility.

THE IMPACT OF SOCIAL MEDIA

Social media, such as Facebook, Twitter, and Instagram, did not exist in the early days of the internet, but are a part of many people's daily lives today. This relatively new technology has had both positive and negative impacts on the lives of LGBTQ people, particularly young people.

> On one hand, social media allows modern LGBTQ people to befriend one another, even from a distance.

This can help them build networks of emotional support, where they can share their struggles among people who understand. However, social media also presents an opportunity for homophobic, transphobic and queerphobic people to harass LGBTQ people. This harassment is called cyberbullying, and can take many forms.

According to GLSEN (Gay, Lesbian & Straight Education Network), 42 percent of LGBTQ youth have experienced cyberbullying. The rate of cyberbullying is three times higher for LGBTQ youth than non-LGBTQ youth.[1]

For minority groups such as LGBTQ people, the internet was an incredibly helpful new tool.

In some cases, LGBTQ people can face physical danger due to cyberbullying. Bullies may "out" their victims, sharing their victim's sexual orientation or gender identity with people who they know might harm the victim. Some LGBTQ people have been bullied so heavily online that they have committed suicide due to the humiliation, physical danger, and/or feelings of hopelessness that the bullying caused.

Cyberbullying is a serious issue, especially when it comes to LGBTQ young people, who are already at a higher risk for discrimination and violence.

Nevertheless, for many activists, the new avenues of communication offered by the internet provided the opportunity to organize in ways previously only dreamed of. Let's look at just one example, the Transgender Law Center.

THE TRANSGENDER LAW CENTER

In 2002, the Transgender Law Center (TLC) opened in California. This organization advocated for transgender rights. It also helped to connect transgender people who'd had their rights violated because of their gender identity with lawyers and other legal service providers who understood transgender issues.

Eventually, TLC went on to become the largest transgender-led civil rights organization in the United States. But its success might not have been possible without the growing communications technology of the early 2000s.

AN IMPORTANT RULING

In 2004, a transgender woman named Diane Schroer was hired to work as a terrorism specialist for the Congressional Research Service at the Library of Congress in Washington, DC.[6] Diane was chosen because of her extensive background and experience. Before Diane began her new job, she told her employer that she was transgender and would be medically transitioning. In response, her employer fired her. Diane filed a discrimination lawsuit and in 2008, a judge ruled that the Library of Congress had violated the Civil Rights Act by discriminating against her.

TLC was cofounded by Dylan Vade, a Stanford University law graduate and transgender man, and his colleague, Chris Daley. While practicing law, Dylan recognized a need for better legal representation for transgender people.

In one interview, he said, "I've been studying the law for three years and I don't see myself in any of the cases—or if I do, I'm called a freak. The problems surrounding transgender issues are so blatant and obvious in the law, it makes me want to change it." By forming TLC, Dylan hoped to accomplish this goal.

TLC launched a website and blog in the early 2000s. At the time, many organizations did not have websites and blogs were a very new way to spread information. Because of TLC's decision to take advantage of the internet, people from all over the world could easily connect with the organization and the resources it provided. The public could also follow TLC's blog for news about issues affecting transgender people nationwide. This helped the organization grow and gain public support.

In 2003, TLC helped revise San Francisco's regulations on gender identity discrimination, adding language to help the city be more inclusive of people who did not identify as male or female. That same year, TLC helped pass legislation in the city of Oakland, California, that banned gender identity discrimination in housing, employment, and city services. Since then, TLC has been involved in many more cases that affected the rights of transgender and nonbinary people in the United States.

A HISTORIC VISIT

The White House, in Washington, DC, is more than the home of the president of the United States and the first family. The White House also hosts many events, such as charity dinners and national holiday celebrations.

In 2003, the White House hosted a class reunion for the Yale University class of 1968, from which then-President George W. Bush (1946–) had graduated. A transgender woman named Petra Leilani Akwai attended the event, making her the first openly transgender person ever officially welcomed into the White House.[4]

In an interview with *The New York Times*, Petra said that she found the president to be welcoming when she told him that she was transgender.

"I was dressed in an evening dress . . . and I said, 'Hello, George.' And in order for him not to be confused, in case he hadn't been briefed, because our class was all male, I said, 'I guess the last time we spoke, I was still living as a man.' And he said, 'But now you're you.' He leaned forward and gave me a little sort of smile. I thought it was a sincere thing, and it was very charming."

Although President George W. Bush did not support many LGBTQ rights, such as the right for same-sex couples to marry, it was encouraging for the American LGBTQ community to see the leader of the United States officially welcome a transgender person to the White House. For many, it was a symbol that LGBTQ people of all kinds were becoming more accepted in mainstream society.

TAKING TO THE STREETS

In June 2004, San Francisco held its largest-ever transgender pride parade, called the Trans March. This march symbolized a new era of transgender acceptance within the LGBTQ community. It's hard to imagine that just a few decades earlier, Sylvia Rivera, Marsha P. Johnson, and other transgender people had not been welcome to march in New York, even within New York's LGBTQ Pride Parade!

> The Trans March began after an anonymous email was sent to several local activists in San Francisco.

The email suggested that a march should take place specifically for "those with other labels for themselves and no labels for themselves, those who see gender as having more than two options, and those who live between the existing options." The writer laid out clear goals for the march, saying that it would be a public way to "support one another as a community, through all of our struggles; to speak out against violence, hate, transphobia, and the oppression of any and all of us under the existing social structure; and to be fabulous and powerful in the company of others that are fabulous and powerful."[5]

A BOOST IN ADVOCACY

Advocacy organizations and civil rights organizations help connect people who have been or might be discriminated against with resources that can help them. Like the TLC, many transgender advocacy organizations were founded in the early 2000s. The Sylvia Rivera Law Project, founded in 2002, provides free legal resources to low-income transgender, intersex, and nonbinary people. The Transgender Legal Defense and Education Fund, founded in 2003, provides education on transgender rights and direct legal services for transgender people. The Center of Excellence for Transgender Health, founded in 2007, puts on programs to address the health concerns of transgender people in different communities. Why is advocacy so important?

Several hundred people participated in the first march, which started in Dolores Park and continued to the civic center more than two miles away. The parade soon became an annual tradition, and it still takes place in San Francisco every year.

Although the first Trans March did not center around a specific political cause, marches since then have included moments of silence for murdered transgender people and speeches about specific discriminatory policies and laws. In 2004, a mistrial was declared in the murder trial of three men accused of murdering transgender teenager Gwen Araujo (1985–2002). Since then, honoring Gwen's memory has been an important part of the Trans March.[7]

Today, the Trans March is the largest transgender pride event in the United States. About 10,000 people attend the march every year, and other cities around the world have followed in San Francisco's footsteps, hosting Trans March events of their own.

AN AMERICAN FIRST

As more people became aware of transgender and nonbinary people, several firsts occurred that made it seem as though American society was increasing its tolerance for these communities. Crucially, these events demonstrated a new level of acceptance.

In November of 2008, Stu Rasmussen (1948–) was elected mayor in the small city of Silverton, Oregon. Stu had already been elected as mayor twice before, once in 1988 and again in 1990, and served on Silverton's city council. But 2008 was different. This time Stu was elected after coming out as transgender, making Stu the first openly transgender mayor in the United States.[8]

Watch a video of Diane Schroer speaking about transgender discrimination and her life growing up, as well as her own court case.

Schroer transgender case

Stu, who uses the pronoun "he/she," lived and worked in Silverton his/her entire life, and had always been active in the community. In addition to serving as mayor, Stu served as a member of the Silverton City Council and the Silver Falls Library Board and operated several small businesses in Silverton, including a local cable company. During high school, Stu worked at a local one-screen movie theater, the Palace Theater. As an adult, Stu operates the Palace Theater along with his/her business partner, Roger Paulson. Stu's family and community were largely supportive of his/her gender identity and medical transition.

Stu has become a small-town transgender icon. He/she is known for having a relaxed attitude when it comes to his/her identity. On Stu's website, he/she describes election as mayor in 2008 as "no big deal."

Stu Rasmussen

credit: Our Town/Brenna Wiegand

> "When I won, it was 'no big deal' here in Silverton, but for some reason that election attracted a lot of attention elsewhere."

Stu also notes that he/she was surprised to have been America's first transgender mayor. "I just happen to be transgendered—something I didn't even know the word for until I discovered it on the internet. I've been a cross-dresser or transvestite my whole life, only 'coming out' recently and thereby discovering that life goes on very nicely. Apparently, I'm the first openly transgendered mayor of any U.S. city—although there are [trans] people serving in public office around the world, this was a 'first' for the USA. Well, I guess somebody had to do it!"[9]

In 2010, Stu was re-elected mayor of Silverton. Stu describes himself/herself as socially progressive, fiscally conservative, and focused on making sure that Silverton remains a well-run, small city with responsible government spending.

A CELEBRITY PIONEER

In 2009, Chaz Bono (1969–), child of famous singers Cher (1946–) and the late Sonny Bono (1935–1998), publicly revealed his gender identity as a transgender man. In 2011, Chaz decided to appear on the popular reality television series, *Dancing with the Stars*.

Chaz had experienced gender dysphoria from an early age. In an interview with *The Sun*, Chaz said "As far back as four or five I felt like a boy and wished I was a boy. At that time I didn't know anything about people being transgender or changing their sex." In 1995, Chaz came out to his family as a lesbian.

Even though Chaz's mother, Cher, was famous for supporting LGBTQ rights, Chaz said that Cher was not completely supportive at first. "My mother is a gay icon, yet she wasn't over the moon when I came out as a lesbian in 1995. I wasn't surprised by her reaction. In fact, I knew it was going to be bad," Chaz said.

> According to Chaz, his mother also had a hard time accepting his gender identity when he came out as transgender in 2009. However, she eventually grew to accept him.

"As it goes on I think she feels more comfortable with me as Chaz. If I'm taking flak in the press or people are being mean on Twitter, Cher will jump to my defense. She sticks up for me—and what an ally to have. We are developing a new relationship," Chaz said, in his interview with *The Sun*.

In 2011, Chaz announced that he would compete on the 13th season of *Dancing with the Stars*. Chaz's appearance on the show was important to many LGBTQ Americans because transgender people, as is true for people from other minority groups, are not seen very often on popular television shows. Because of this, the public doesn't have many chances to get to know or relate to transgender people.

Chaz Bono at the GLAAD Awards 2012

Chaz's appearance on *Dancing with the Stars* also caused controversy. Some people boycotted the show, wrote angry letters to the broadcasting network, and even threatened Chaz online. But Chaz also gained many fans during the 13th season.

VOCAB LAB 📖

Write down what you think each word means. What root words can you find to help you? What does the context of the word tell you?

advocacy, **cyberbullying**, **legislation**, **marginalized**, **niche**, and **technology**.

Compare your definitions with those of your friends or classmates. Did you all come up with the same meanings? Turn to the text and glossary if you need help.

It also means that young transgender people don't always have role models to look up to. Chaz Bono's appearance on *Dancing with the Stars* represented an important step for transgender people in the media. Many Americans took it as a sign that transgender people were becoming more accepted in society.

In 2011, the same year that he appeared on *Dancing with the Stars*, Chaz released a documentary about his life and medical transition, called *Becoming Chaz*. Today, Chaz often speaks in support of transgender causes on social media and at LGBTQ events around the world.

For people who felt lonely and marginalized, the internet was something of a lifesaver. For organizations working to advance the cause of LGBTQ rights and plan events such as the Trans March, it was a huge boon in terms of research and widespread communication and marketing. Even as an increase in publicity meant a backlash in some areas, the improved communications helped many.

In the next chapter, we'll look at how the fictional world of literature, television, and theater has portrayed transgender and nonbinary people.

KEY QUESTIONS

- Many positive legal changes occurred for the U.S. transgender community during the early 2000s. How did the internet contribute to these changes? Do you think these steps forward would have happened without the internet?

- Could San Francisco's 2004 Trans March have been easily organized in an earlier decade? Why or why not?

- How has the internet been a negative part of the LGBTQ experience? In your view, does the good outweigh the bad or vice versa?

IN THE SPOTLIGHT

In 2008, Stu Rasmussen became the first transgender mayor in the United States. This was a big moment for the transgender community, as it gained representation in an important sphere—politics. What have the repercussions of this first step been?

- **Research other openly transgender elected officials throughout the world.** How many have there been since 2008? Were any openly transgender officials elected to public office outside of the United States before 2008? Note your findings.

- **Discuss with friends or classmates your predictions for the future of transgender officials in the United States and around the world.**

  - Do you think there will be many more to come? Why or why not?

  - Do you believe that such officials will always be considered controversial? Why or why not?

  - Will their numbers ever be equal or similar to the number of cisgender officials? Why or why not?

To investigate more, research the basics of writing a campaign speech, then write a speech as if you were running for political office. What is your platform? What issues are important to you? Do you think it would be challenging to convince voters to support your platform? What additional challenges might transgender and nonbinary people face when running for public office?

Chapter 6

Gender Identity in Popular Media

HEY, SOMEONE LIKE ME!!

How have transgender people been represented in works of fiction?

Books, television, and movies often reflect a society's culture by telling stories and featuring characters that fit a culture's current ideals. When we look at the history of transgender people in media, we can find a long, winding path that closely follows the actual history of transgender and nonbinary people in American culture.

Do you have a favorite work of fiction? Do you remember how you felt when you read or watched it for the first time? Fiction is a very powerful medium for individuals and communities of people. Remember how people reacted when they saw Chaz Bono in *Dancing with the Stars*? Had that show been a work of fiction instead of a reality show, it might have spawned the same kinds of reactions in viewers.

The late 1990s and early 2000s were a time of great change for LGBTQ people in the United States. New technology was making it easier for LGBTQ people to connect with one another and organize together. Because of this, the LGBTQ community was more visible than ever in mainstream American culture. More people were seeing LGBTQ people and thinking about the issues they faced.

As a result, more fictional stories about LGBTQ people began to be produced, especially on television.

You can know a lot about a culture by reading current books or watching current television shows. Media can also help change culture by telling stories that help readers or viewers reflect on a culture's flaws. Let's examine how this has worked for LGBTQ people.

A REFLECTION OF CHANGE

In 1994, the sitcom *Friends* aired for the first time. This show would go on to become one of the most popular television sitcoms of all time. The first episodes of the show introduced an openly lesbian character named Carol Willick. Eventually, *Friends* went on to portray a long-term lesbian relationship between Carol and her partner, Susan Bunch.

> The two characters became parents together and got married, even though same-sex marriage was not legal yet in the real world.

In 1997, the popular sitcom, *Ellen*, first aired. The show starred actress and stand-up comic Ellen DeGeneres (1958–) as the character Ellen Morgan. The character came out as a lesbian on the show, the first time that a sitcom had ever shown a character coming out. This television milestone occurred while the real Ellen DeGeneres announced that she was lesbian.

In 1998, a sitcom called *Will & Grace* first aired. *Will & Grace* featured the friendship between a gay man and straight woman. An important supporting character was also a gay man. The show grew to be one of the most popular sitcoms on television, running until 2006. It was even re-booted in 2017.

GENDER WONDER

Media representation, or the portrayal of certain kinds of people in media, is important—it can help cement our sense of self to see characters who are like us. Cisgender people can watch or read about plenty of cisgender characters. But transgender and nonbinary people do not get as much media representation. Luckily, many works of fiction today are working to address this problem.

You may be surprised to learn that one of the first movies to feature a transgender main character was made in the 1950s. The 1954 French film *Adam est . . . Eve* is the story of a professional boxer who realizes that she is a transgender woman and decides to medically transition.[1] The film contains some jokes and ideas about transgender people that would be considered very offensive today. However, it does portray a transgender person who is happy with the results of her transition. The film also has a happy ending—the main character finds love in a relationship with a transgender man. This movie was an important moment in film history and in the history of transgender people.

Even as gay and lesbian characters began to appear more frequently on television in the 1990s and early 2000s, transgender and nonbinary characters were rarely seen. However, transgender and nonbinary characters had historically been present in other forms of fiction, even before the 1990s.

A MUCH-LOVED MUSICAL

Rent is a 1993 rock musical about a group of struggling young friends living in New York City during the late 1980s. Most of the main characters in *Rent* are LGBTQ, including one character named Angel Dumott Schunard, who frequently cross-dresses. Angel is referred to as a drag queen, and usually uses female pronouns to refer to herself.

> It is unclear whether Angel would consider herself transgender by modern standards.

Rent focuses on themes of love, acceptance, poverty, mortality, and friendship. The characters all have their own ways of dealing with the struggles of life. Angel Dumott Schunard is portrayed as a happy, generous, mothering character who deeply appreciates the love she has found with her boyfriend, Tom Collins, a part-time professor at New York University.

Both Angel and Tom have AIDS, but Angel remains upbeat and kind in the face of a disease that meant near-certain death in the 1980s. She is shown to be a capable, brave character who is willing to stand up for others and seek help for her personal issues through group therapy sessions. This is important, since early works of fiction usually portrayed LGBTQ characters as depressed or angry people.

In *Rent*, Angel eventually dies of AIDS, but her death serves to change her friends' outlooks on life and love. At Angel's funeral, one friend describes how Angel once stood up to a man who was harassing her for cross-dressing, telling him, "I'm more of a man than you'll ever be; I'm more of a woman than you'll ever get." Another friend describes a time when Angel helped a frightened, out-of-town family with directions and happily posed for a picture with them. After the funeral, Tom remarks that, "Angel helped us believe in love."

Rent premiered on Broadway in 1996. The show won various awards during its Broadway run, including four Tony Awards. In 2005, the musical was made into a movie.

Rent's Broadway run lasted until 2008. Throughout that time, *Rent*'s producers sometimes sold tickets for the first two rows of the theater for only $20 each, a fraction of the regular price. This way, more people could afford to see the show, including people struggling with poverty, like the characters in *Rent*. The low ticket prices helped grow *Rent*'s large, loyal fan base. The musical's widespread success helped increase mainstream awareness of many issues facing the American LGBTQ community, including HIV and AIDS, disproportionate poverty, and discrimination.

LA BOHÈME

Rent is loosely based on the 1896 opera *La Bohème* by Giacomo Puccini (1858–1924). In the opera, a group of struggling young artists have to deal with a plague of tuberculosis that is sweeping through their city of Paris, France. The characters in *Rent* also have a plague to deal with in the form of HIV, the virus that causes AIDS.

Watch one of the most iconic songs from *Rent* at this website. Why was this such an important cultural moment in LGBTQ history?

🔍 Rent musical seasons

TELEVISION HISTORY

In 1975, the popular television sitcom *The Jeffersons* aired for the first time. The show focused on the lives of an African American couple, George and Louise Jefferson. *The Jeffersons* was most famous for dealing with issues of race and racial prejudice in America.

Although the show was lighthearted most of the time, it did also contain episodes focusing on alcoholism, suicide, and other serious topics. One episode in the show's fourth season dealt with gender identity.

In this episode, called "Once A Friend," George hears that an old friend named Eddie Stokes is passing through New York. George and Eddie served together in the Navy during the Korean War. What George doesn't know is that Eddie is a transgender woman named Edie, and that she has medically transitioned since George last saw her. George is upset, but eventually comes to understand that he hasn't lost his friend.

"Once a Friend" was one of the first times a transgender character appeared on television. The episode also allowed Edie to tell her own story. How might the story have been different if Edie was turned away by her old friend instead of finally being welcomed?

CHILDREN'S LITERATURE

Until recently, children's literature included very few transgender characters. What might it be like to be a transgender or nonbinary young person, unable to find any books about people like yourself?

As cultures have become more accepting of transgender people, more transgender characters are beginning to appear in children's literature.

10,000 Dresses is a children's picture book published in 2008 about a transgender girl named Bailey. Each night, Bailey dreams of dresses.

Some of these dresses are magical, such as a dress made of windows that show landmarks from around the world. Each morning, Bailey asks her family to help her find the dress she dreamed about.

At first, Bailey's family is not accepting of her desire to wear dresses. They tell her that she is a boy, and her brother even calls her "gross." But Bailey makes friends with a woman who lives across the street, and together they make a beautiful dress for Bailey. *10,000 Dresses* is a story that shows that anyone should be able to wear what they want, and that acceptance can always be found somewhere.

Meet Polkadot is the first in a series of children's picture books, published in 2014, about a child named Polkadot who is both transgender and nonbinary. Polkadot doesn't identify as male or female and has socially transitioned to express their gender identity. *Meet Polkadot* explains how Polkadot feels about the world around them, and the challenges they face in different places, such as bathrooms, clothing stores, and more.

Polkadot has several friends their own age who accept them and learn about the world from Polkadot's perspective. Polkadot's story encourages children to think outside the gender binary and accept the identities of those around them.

George is a middle-grade novel by Alex Gino, published in 2015, that tells the story of a transgender middle-school girl named George. George knows she is transgender, but at first is afraid to come out.

However, when her teacher refuses to let her try out for a female part in the class play, George and her best friend, Kelly, come up with a plan for George to come out. *George* is a story that shows the importance of inclusion for transgender children, and how rewarding it can be to overcome fears.

COMICS AND GRAPHIC NOVELS

Comic books, which tell short stories with both illustrations and words, have been around since the 1800s. They rose to popularity in the late 1930s, when Superman Comics were first published, and have remained popular since.

Transgender characters have been appearing in comics since at least the 1980s, when the comic series *Camelot 3000* featured a male character who was reincarnated as a woman. This character still identifies as male and eventually changes his name from Amber to Sir Tristan.

In 2013, in the modern *Batgirl* comics, a character named Alysia Yeoh comes out to Batgirl as a transgender woman.

This character is Batgirl's friend and roommate. Several graphic novels have also featured transgender characters. Many of these graphic novels are for older teenage or adult readers. Be sure to check with an adult before choosing a graphic novel or comic to read.

A CARTOON BREAKTHROUGH

Steven Universe is an animated children's television series featuring a race of genderless aliens called "gems." The show follows the story of a 14-year-old, half-gem, half-human boy named Steven Universe as he attempts to get a handle on his own magic powers while defending the earth from gem-related threats. The show has become well-known for its varied portrayal of gender and LGBTQ relationships.

In *Steven Universe*, gems use she/her pronouns. They are also voiced by female voice actors. So, while gems are technically genderless, many fans of the show generally view the romantic relationships between gems as lesbian relationships. The shows creator, Rebecca Sugar, describes the gems as nonbinary women.[3]

Steven Universe has spent several seasons delving into the relationships between gems who love one another. In the 2018 episode "Reunited," two gems named Ruby and Sapphire married one another. The episode marked the first time a same-sex wedding had been shown in a children's animated show.

Gems in *Steven Universe* have the power to magically fuse with one another, creating an entirely new gem with a personality all her own.

THE LEFT HAND OF DARKNESS

The Left Hand of Darkness is a 1976 science fiction novel by Ursula K. Le Guin (1929–2018). It is the story of a man named Ai, from a planet called Terra, who is sent on a political mission to a planet called Gethen. The people of Gethen have no fixed gender. Their gender changes from time to time, based on the circumstances around them. Because of this, Gethenians live in a world without sexual prejudice and without strict cultural roles for men and women. Estraven, a Gethenian who becomes a friend of Ai, is shown to have both masculine and feminine qualities. The story is meant to show that all beings, regardless of where they're from, need both masculine and feminine qualities to survive. *The Left Hand of Darkness* won a Nebula Award and a Hugo Award for excellence in science fiction, making Ursula K. Le Guin the first female author to win both awards.

You can watch a clip of Stevonnie fusing for the first time at this website.

Steven and Connie Fuse

Gems formed in this way are called "fusions." For example, Ruby and Sapphire form a fusion named Garnet. In the 2015 episode "Alone Together," Steven fuses with his female human friend, Connie. Together, they form a fusion named Stevonnie. Because Stevonnie possesses a combination of Steven's and Connie's physical traits, Stevonnie is physically intersex.

Although Stevonnie never talks about their gender identity specifically, they use they/them pronouns, implying to viewers that they are nonbinary. It is also worth noting that other characters, whether male or female, generally regard Stevonnie as cool and beautiful.

> Such universal support for a nonbinary character in children's media is revolutionary.

Steven Universe was created by Rebecca Sugar (1987–), a bisexual, nonbinary woman. Rebecca is the first woman to independently create a series for Cartoon Network.

Rebecca Sugar on a conference panel

When asked about Stevonnie's gender during an interview in 2015, Rebecca responded, "Stevonnie is an experience! The living relationship between Steven and Connie. What I love about Stevonnie is that we are working with a metaphor that is so complex and so specific but also really, really relatable, in the form of a character. Stevonnie challenges gender norms as an individual, but also serves as a metaphor for all the terrifying firsts in a first relationship."[4]

Fiction can reflect culture or even help to change it. For decades, books, movies, plays, and television shows have portrayed transgender and nonbinary characters, from award-winning science fiction masterpieces such as *The Left Hand of Darkness* to current children's television shows such as *Steven Universe*. These characters can help more people learn about real-life transgender and nonbinary people, and they reflect the changing cultural attitudes about them.

In the next chapter, we'll discuss cultural changes toward transgender and nonbinary people in the second decade of the twenty-first century, from famous figures to landmark legal decisions.

VOCAB LAB

Write down what you think each word means. What root words can you find to help you? What does the context of the word tell you?

criticize, feminine, fiction, homophobia, literature, masculine, and **stereotype.**

Compare your definitions with those of your friends or classmates. Did you all come up with the same meanings? Turn to the text and glossary if you need help.

KEY QUESTIONS

- Why was the appearance of Chandler Bing's father on *Friends* met with praise by some and criticism by others? Can you think of other controversial LGBTQ characters?

- Why is it important that children read books and watch movies and shows that include portrayals of all kinds of people? What would the world be like if only one kind of person appeared in fiction?

BY THE BOOK

Books with transgender and nonbinary characters have become more common in recent years, including books for kids. How are these characters portrayed? Are they still relatable, even to readers who are not transgender or nonbinary?

- **Choose a book, written for young people, that features a transgender or nonbinary character.** You could choose a picture book, such as *10,000 Dresses* by Marcus Ewert or *Meet Polkadot* by Talcott Broadhead. You could also choose a novel, such as *George* by Alex Gino or *Gracefully Grayson* by Ami Polonsky. Read the book and take notes on how the character is portrayed. What is the character like? What are their passions and problems? Are they much different from other characters in other books you have read?

- **Now meet with someone who read a different book than you did.** What differences do you see between your two characters? What traits do your characters share, and what traits, if any, do you and your partner share with your two characters?

> **To investigate more,** watch an episode of a show for young people featuring LGBTQ characters, such as *Steven Universe* or *Danger and Eggs*. How do the characters in these shows compare with the characters you read about earlier? Do you learn as much about characters by watching them as you do reading about them? How do you prefer to consume stories, by reading, by watching, or both? Why?

Chapter 7
The "New" Revolution

WE'RE HERE TO BE OURSELVES, AND WE ALWAYS HAVE BEEN!

What issues do transgender and nonbinary people face today?

Transgender and nonbinary people are more visible in American society than ever. Their visibility means they have more opportunity to feel connected and supported. It also means that society can recognize the history and contributions of transgender people and ensure that we continue working for legal and political equality in this country.

In the United States and some other Western cultures, transgender and nonbinary people are continuing to be more accepted in mainstream culture. This is a result of ongoing activism and advocacy, helped by new technology that has allowed transgender and nonbinary people to better connect with one another while becoming more publicly visible.

Because of this new visibility, many people are now hearing more about transgender and nonbinary people than they ever have before. More transgender and nonbinary people are coming out publicly. They appear more than ever in media such as books and television shows.

In reality, transgender and nonbinary people have always been a part of human history. They have always faced discrimination in certain cultures, which has led to violence against them as well as other obstacles. As acceptance for transgender and nonbinary people grows, they will continue to be more visible.

A TRANSGENDER SUPERSTAR

In 2010, actress Laverne Cox made history as the first African American transgender woman to produce and star in her own television show, VH1's *TRANSform Me*. The reality show featured Laverne and two other transgender women surprising cisgender women with makeovers. In 2014, Laverne was nominated for a Primetime Emmy Award, making her the first openly transgender person to be nominated for an Emmy Award in the acting category. *TRANSform Me* is for older teenage or adult viewers. Be sure to check with an adult before watching.

Several prominent magazines, including *Variety* and *Time*, have featured Laverne on their covers. In fact, in 2014, Laverne Cox became the first openly transgender person to be featured on the cover of *Time* magazine.[1] In a 2015 interview with *Rolling Stone*, Laverne was asked how she felt about the headline on her *Variety* magazine cover, which read "Hollywood Trans Formation."[2]

> "I think what's important and moving . . . about naming the trans piece is that trans people are not always visible. For decades we were told that we needed to transition, blend in and disappear as transgender people. And then there's a lot of folks who don't think we *really* exist; they insist that we are always and only the gender we were assigned at birth. So the process of naming that identity and claiming one's trans-ness, in a world that tells us we should not exist—that feels revolutionary. It feels like a very important step."

In 2015, Laverne produced a documentary called *Laverne Cox Presents: The T Word*, in which seven transgender people, ages 12 to 24, told their own stories. Laverne narrated the documentary and conducted the interviews.

It's easy to imagine how a person who has only recently heard about the issues that transgender and nonbinary people face could wrongly assume that such issues are a new phenomenon.

GENDER WONDER

Why are the issues facing transgender and nonbinary people often portrayed as "new" issues, even though transgender and nonbinary people have existed throughout human history?

She went on to win a Daytime Emmy Award for her work on the documentary, making her the first openly transgender woman to win the award as an executive producer.

During a 2015 interview with *The Guardian*, Laverne described her childhood as being difficult and full of bullying due to her gender identity. She said, however, that dancing and acting helped her through, and led her to her current success. "I'm a black transgender chick from Mobile, Alabama, I grew up poor and working class, and I'm on the cover of magazines," Laverne said.

HISTORY-MAKING MEMOS

In 2011, the U.S. Department of Justice released a memo—a formal, written letter—that offered guidance about how federal agencies should treat transgender employees. The memo stated that Title VII of the federal Civil Rights Act prohibited workplace discrimination against transgender employees.[3] This was the first memo specifically addressing transgender rights that the Department of Justice had ever sent.

In 2016, the Department of Justice and the U.S. Department of Education released a joint memo that offered guidance for public schools on how to honor the rights of transgender students. The memo stated that under Title IX of the Education Amendments Act, public schools must not discriminate against transgender students. According to the memo, if a public school was found to be discriminating against transgender students, that school could lose its federal funding.

The memo also outlined other groundbreaking rules regarding transgender students, which the federal government had never before addressed. For example, the memo stated that schools should call transgender students by their preferred pronouns and preferred names, even if their education records or IDs stated different names. According to the memo, every transgender student also had the right to use whichever bathroom and locker room was consistent with their gender identity and to join gender-specific athletic teams consistent with their gender identity.[4]

> In the United States, federal agencies tend to change as new presidents appoint new federal employees. This can lead to changes in policy.

Both the 2011 and 2016 memos on transgender rights were issued during the presidency of Barack Obama (1961–). In January 2017, Donald Trump (1946–) became the 45th president of the United States. His administration appointed new federal employees in a variety of agencies. This led to changes in how the Department of Justice interpreted certain laws, such as the federal Civil Rights Act and the Education Amendments Act.

In 2017, the Department of Justice released a new memo. It stated that the federal Civil Rights Act did not protect transgender employees from discrimination on the basis of gender identity— the opposite of what had been stated in the 2011 memo. Also in 2017, the Department of Justice and the Department of Education withdrew the guidelines that had been outlined in the 2016 memo to public schools.

CHRISTINE HALLQUIST

Christine Hallquist made history in 2018, when she became the first openly transgender major party nominee for governor in the United States. Christine ran as a Democrat in the 2018 election for governor of Vermont. Her platform included raising the minimum hourly wage in Vermont to $15 and connecting every Vermont home and business with fiber optic cable, among other issues.

Even though the Department of Justice and the Department of Education no longer interpret the law in the same way they did when the 2011 and 2016 memos were released, the original memos still made history. These memos showed that the federal government had been willing to address the issues facing transgender and nonbinary people. The precedence is set for a different administration to do so again in the future.

BATHROOMS: AN UNLIKELY BATTLEGROUND

Imagine that you are a student who needs to use the bathroom. You are a girl, but if you use the girl's bathroom, you'll get in trouble. You might be sent to the principal's office or get kicked out of school.

Now, imagine that you are a gender other than male or female. You're a nonbinary student, but your school has only two bathrooms—the boys' room and the girls' room. You'll likely feel uncomfortable if you use either one, and others might judge you for not belonging in the bathroom, whichever one you decide to use. These are situations that transgender and nonbinary people face every day—not just in schools but in restaurants, offices, and other public places. Bathrooms have become an unlikely battleground when it comes to the civil rights of transgender and nonbinary people.

In the United States, laws and ordinances that decide who can use which bathroom vary widely from state to state and city to city. In one city, it might be okay for a transgender person to use the bathroom that matches their gender identity, but if they drive into a different city, they may be required by law to use a different bathroom.

You can read the wording in the 2016 memo about schools at this website. How might your community have reacted to this news?

 gov 2016 transgender

GENDER WONDER

Why do you think that some people feel so strongly about who can use which public restrooms? Why would being forced to use the wrong public restroom cause a person to feel unsafe?

If they don't know these laws or find it too humiliating or dangerous to use a bathroom that doesn't match their gender identity, they could face arrest.

What makes it dangerous to use a certain bathroom? Transphobia and queerphobia. Unfortunately, transgender and nonbinary people are still subjected to disproportionate amounts of discrimination and violence, so they don't always want to draw attention to their gender identity in public. It's an issue of safety.

If a transgender woman is forced to use the men's restroom, or vice versa, or if a nonbinary person is forced into either restroom, that draws attention to their gender identity. Transphobic, homophobic, and queerphobic strangers could take notice and show their objections through bullying, intimidation, and violence. Does this sound like a fair choice to force someone to make?

Breaking the law comes with its own dangers. If a transgender or nonbinary person is arrested for using the wrong restroom, they may face danger at the hands of police officers who are transphobic or queerphobic.

Many jails hold prisoners in separate areas based on perceived gender. In many cases, prison authorities examine prisoners' bodies and separate prisoners based on their physical appearance alone. So, for example, a person with a penis can be placed in an area for male prisoners, regardless of their gender identity. This means that a transgender woman, who lives and dresses as a woman, may be placed in a holding cell with male prisoners. It is easy to imagine how this could lead to physical or sexual violence.

FAR-REACHING CONSEQUENCES

Laws that prohibit transgender and nonbinary people from using certain bathrooms are dangerous for everyone. How can someone such as a store or restaurant manager determine whether someone walking into a public bathroom is transgender or not? What if a woman is mistaken for a man, or vice versa? How are people supposed to stop themselves from being targeted as using the "wrong" restroom?

These laws designating bathroom use, which are sometimes called "bathroom bills," can also impact cisgender people. People of all genders can look different from what society views as typical. For example, in 2015, a cisgender woman named Cortney Bogorad was forcefully pulled out of a women's restroom in Detroit, Michigan, by a security guard who assumed she was a man.[5] People who don't match society's conceptions of gender could be harassed, assaulted, or publicly humiliated by having to publicly prove that they are legally female or male.

Some businesses and schools have begun to install gender-neutral restrooms, which anyone can use. This doesn't completely solve the problems that transgender and nonbinary people face because of bathroom bills.

> But gender-neutral bathrooms do provide more options and more access for people who prefer to choose their own bathroom.

As of 2018, 16 states—Alabama, Arkansas, Illinois, Kansas, Kentucky, Minnesota, Missouri, Montana, New York, South Carolina, South Dakota, Tennessee, Texas, Virginia, Washington, and Wyoming—have considered legislation that would restrict access to public bathrooms, locker rooms, and other sex-segregated facilities. None of this legislation has been passed yet, and some of these states have already rejected the legislation. However, some of the states listed above could still pass the legislation.

North Carolina is the only state that has passed a bathroom bill. The law, called HB2, was passed in 2016. It stated that a person's physical sex had to match the bathroom they used, regardless of their gender identity.

In 2017, North Carolina passed another bill. This bill repealed the state-wide restrictions of HB2. But it also stated that cities in North Carolina could not pass their own anti-discrimination ordinances to protect transgender and nonbinary people.

Some cities, universities, and states have also passed laws or ordinances that protect the right of transgender and nonbinary people to use the bathroom of their choice.

As of 2018, 18 states, plus the District of Columbia, have passed such laws. Those states are California, Colorado, Connecticut, Delaware, Hawaii, Illinois, Iowa, Maine, Maryland, Massachusetts, Minnesota, Nevada, New Jersey, New Mexico, Oregon, Rhode Island, Vermont, and Washington.

GENDER WONDER

Why is it important that more public figures, such as actors, singers, athletes and elected officials, are coming out as transgender and nonbinary than ever before? What impacts might this have on LGBTQ rights in the future?

CONTINUING VIOLENCE

Around the world, transgender and nonbinary people still face disproportionate violence because of their gender identities. In 2017, 28 transgender or nonbinary Americans were killed because of their gender identity.[6] Countries such as Iraq, Iran, Honduras, Uganda, and Russia record high murder rates for transgender and nonbinary people.[7]

> In the United States, transgender and nonbinary people of color face the highest risk of violence. Of the 28 transgender and nonbinary Americans killed in 2017, 21 were people of color.

In 2017, the Trans People of Color Coalition and the Human Rights Campaign (HRC) Foundation released a report detailing the epidemic of violence against transgender people, including the stories of many transgender murder victims. The purpose of the report was to bring more public awareness to the violence transgender people face and to the deadly consequences of transphobia and queerphobia.

Some organizations have created programs that they hope will help decrease the amount of violence against transgender and nonbinary people. Such programs include educational workshops for schools, police departments, and domestic violence shelters to increase knowledge about transgender issues. The National Center for Transgender Equality, the National LGBTQ Task Force, and Parity are just three organizations aiming to decrease violence against transgender and nonbinary people in the United States.

In the United States, the second decade of the twenty-first century has seen more cultural changes toward transgender and nonbinary people than almost any decade before. The civil rights of transgender and nonbinary people are being openly discussed and cultural attitudes are changing. Celebrities such as Laverne Cox and Caitlyn Jenner are bringing more awareness than ever before to issues of gender identity, even as some states attempt to pass laws that discriminate against them.

What's next? How will future generations view transgender issues? What are some of the solutions that might be applied to the problems transgender and nonbinary people face? How can people become more accepting of those who are different than themselves?

Some people worry about the future of transgender and nonbinary civil rights, while others remain hopeful. Only time will tell how American culture, as well as other cultures around the world, will change in response to the undeniable visibility of transgender and nonbinary people.

You can read the HRC Foundation's report on transgender and nonbinary violence at this website. Why is it important to keep these stories in the eye of the public?

Warning: Some of these stories contain descriptions of violence.

 HRC time to act

KEY QUESTIONS

- Why does it matter when an organization such as the Girl Scouts of America takes a stand for or against the rights of transgender and nonbinary people? How could this organization have handled it better when a transgender girl wanted to join its ranks?

- What kind of impact do celebrities have on transgender and nonbinary issues?

- What do you think it will be like for transgender and nonbinary people in another 10 years?

BIOGRAPHY RESEARCH

At the heart of every social or political movement are the stories of the people who were brave enough to stand up for their rights and the rights of the people around them, despite the threat of violence, exile, personal loss, professional loss, and every other kind of hardship. You've read a lot of stories in this book about the revolutionaries behind the LGBTQ movement for civil rights. Dive deeper into their stories and see what makes them call out injustice when they see it.

- **Choose a transgender, intersex, or nonbinary public figure, either one you've read about in this book or someone who wasn't mentioned.** Try to find answers to the following questions.

  - What was their childhood like?

  - Were they bullied as a young person?

  - Did they have support from their family?

  - How did their life change when they came out to people, if they took this step?

  - How was their professional life affected by their gender identification?

  - What did they do to advance the rights of transgender and nonbinary people?

- **Write a biography of the person you chose.** Include quotes regarding how they feel about their gender identity.

- **Pair up with someone who chose a different public figure than you did.** What similarities can you find between your two public figures?

To investigate more, visit the website of Christine Hallquist, the 2018 Vermont gubernatorial candidate. Read the "about" and "issues" sections of her website and take notes on both. What kinds of events and former occupations in Christine's life do you think have impacted how she feels about certain political issues?

abstract: existing more in thought and ideas than in reality.

activism: working to create social change.

advocacy: public support for or recommendation of a particular cause or policy.

affirm: to state as a fact.

agender: when someone does not identify themselves as having a particular gender.

AIDS (acquired immunodeficiency syndrome): a disease resulting from HIV that attacks the body's immune system.

amend: to change a law.

American Civil Liberties Union (ACLU): an organization founded in 1920 to defend the civil rights of all Americans.

anonymous: not identified by name.

asexual: without sexual feelings or associations.

assault: a violent physical or verbal attack.

authentic: genuine or real.

backlash: a strong negative reaction.

bathroom bill: legislation that defines access to public restrooms by transgender and nonbinary individuals.

bias: a way of looking at or thinking about something that might be wrong or unfair or limiting.

bigender: describing a person whose sense of personal identity encompasses two genders.

bigotry: the practice of having very strong and unreasonable opinions, especially about politics, race, or religion, and refusing to consider other people's opinions.

binary: based on two.

bisexual: sexually attracted to both men and women.

blatant: done openly and unashamedly.

boycott: to refuse to buy, use, or participate in something as a means of protest.

camaraderie: the feeling of trust and friendship among a group of people.

castration: removal of the testicles.

charismatic: having a charming nature that inspires devotion in others.

chromosomes: parts of a cell that contain genes, which are what determine a person's physical characteristics.

cisgender: relating to a person whose gender corresponds with the gender they were assigned at birth.

civil rights: the rights that every person should have regardless of gender, race, religion, or sexual orientation.

coming out: the process by which LGBTQ people begin to share their sexual orientation or gender identity openly with other people.

communications technology: the equipment and programs that provide access to information. Also called information technology.

contemporary: modern, existing now, belonging to the current moment.

controversial: an act or decision that is often disagreed with.

controversy: something that causes a lot of argument or disagreement.

corruption: dishonest actions by those in power.

criticize: to form and express a judgment.

cross-dressing: to wear clothing associated with a different gender.

cryptic: having a meaning that is mysterious or obscure.

culture: the beliefs and way of life of a group of people.

GLOSSARY

cyberbullying: the use of electronic communication to bully a person, usually by sending messages that are intimidating or threatening.

deadname: to refer to someone who has changed their name by their previous name.

defendant: a person who is being sued or accused of a crime.

discrimination: treating people unfairly because of certain characteristics, such as their gender, race, religion, or sexual orientation.

disenfranchised: deprived of power, rights or privileges.

disproportionate: too large or too small in comparison with another population.

drag: a performance in which the performers wear clothing more conventionally worn by another gender.

drag performer: a person who performs regularly in drag shows, sometimes called drag kings or drag queens.

exile: banishment from living in a certain place.

feminine: having qualities that are usually associated with women.

feminism: advocacy for women's rights.

fiction: stories that describe imaginary events and people.

fiscally conservative: a political philosophy relating to reduced government spending and government debt.

fundraiser: an activity to raise money for a cause.

gay: sexually attracted to people of the same sex. This word is usually used to describe men, but may be used to describe women as well.

gender: the behavioral, cultural, or psychological traits typically associated with masculinity and femininity.

gender binary: the classification of sex and gender into two distinct, opposite, and disconnected forms of masculine and feminine.

gender dysphoria: distress arising from a conflict between a person's actual gender and the gender they were assigned at birth.

gender fluid: a person who does not identify themselves as having a fixed gender.

gender identity: a person's internal sense of being male, female, some combination of male and female, or neither male nor female.

gender performance: the way someone shows their gender on a daily basis, through a variety of habits and mannerisms, in order to adhere to cultural norms.

gender identity disorder: an outdated term now known as gender dysphoria.

gender non-conforming: describes a person whose gender identity does not conform to the prevailing ideas or practices of gender.

genderqueer: denoting or relating to a person who does not subscribe to conventional gender distinctions but identifies with neither, both, or a combination of male and female genders.

genitalia: the external organs of the reproductive system, including the penis and vagina.

graphic novel: a novel in comic-strip format.

hate crime: a crime motivated by racial, sexual, or other prejudice, typically one involving violence.

heterosexual: a person who is sexually attracted to people of the opposite gender.

homophobia: dislike or prejudice against homosexual people.

homosexual: a person who is sexually attracted to people of the same gender.

hormone therapy: a form of hormone replacement therapy (HRT) in which sex hormones and other hormonal medications are administered to a transgender or nonbinary person.

hostility: great anger or strong dislike.

human immunodeficiency virus (HIV): a virus that attacks the immune system and can eventually lead to AIDS.

icon: a person or thing that grows to represent a larger idea.

infringe: to limit or undermine.

inhumanely: cruelly or without compassion.

innovator: a person who introduces new methods, ideas, or products.

intersectionality: the interconnected nature of certain social categorizations, such as race, class, and gender, especially as they relate to civil rights.

intersex: a person born with physical anatomy that doesn't allow them to easily be assigned a gender of male or female.

invasive: annoying because of being too close, too noisy, or too involved in people's personal lives.

isolated: to be separate and apart from others.

legislation: laws, considered collectively.

lesbian: a woman who is sexually attracted to women.

LGBTQ: lesbian, gay, bisexual, transgender, queer.

LGBTQ rights movement: a civil rights movement that advocates equal rights for gay men, lesbians, bisexuals, transgender people, and genderqueer or nonbinary people.

literature: written work such as poems, plays, and novels.

marginalized: treated as insignificant or unimportant.

masculine: suggestive of or being in some way like a man.

medically transition: when a person undergoes medical treatments so that their physical characteristics better match their gender identity.

memoir: a narrative based on personal experience.

metaphor: a way to describe something by saying it is something else.

minority: a part of the population that is different or is a smaller group.

misconception: a view or opinion that is incorrect because it is based on faulty thinking or understanding.

mistrial: a trial that is invalid through an error in the proceedings.

narrative: a story or account of events.

niche: a job or activity that you are good at or a place that is very suitable.

nonbinary: gender identities that are not exclusively masculine or feminine.

non-conformist: a person whose behavior or views do not conform to prevailing ideas or practices.

nonprofit: an organization supported by donations whose main mission is to help people, animals, the environment, or other causes.

notoriety: the state of being famous or well known.

novelty: new, original.

null and void: to cancel or make invalid.

offensive: describes something that causes someone to feel deeply hurt, upset, or angry.

ordinance: a law created by a town or city.

outing: to reveal someone else's sexuality or gender identity without permission.

pansexual: not limited in sexual choice with regard to biological sex, gender, or gender identity.

GLOSSARY

phenomenon: something seen or observed.

physical sex: the physical anatomy of an individual's reproductive system and secondary sex characteristics.

picket: to stand or march near a certain place to protest or persuade others not to enter.

plaintiff: a person who brings a case in a court of law.

political: relating to the government or the public affairs of a certain place.

portray: to describe or depict someone or something.

precedent: a decision that serves as a guide for the future.

prejudice: an unfair feeling of dislike for a person or group, usually based on gender, race, or religion.

pronoun: a word that is used instead of a noun. The English pronouns "he" and "she" are gender-specific, third-person personal pronouns. The English pronoun "they" is a gender-neutral, third-person pronoun.

protected class: a group of people qualified for certain protections, by law.

queer: an inclusive term used to identify with the LGBTQ community as a whole. It may also relate to a gender or sexual orientation that does not correspond with established ideas about sexuality and gender.

queerphobia: fear or hatred of queer people, including gay, lesbian, transgender, and genderqueer/nonbinary people.

repeal: to cancel a law.

repercussion: an unintended consequence as the result of an action.

riot: a violent disturbance of the peace by a crowd.

royalty: money paid to an author or artist for each book or other piece of work sold.

science fiction: a fictional story featuring imaginary science and technology.

sex reassignment: surgery to change physical sex.

sexual orientation: a person's sexual identity in relation to the gender to which they are attracted.

shun: to avoid or reject.

sodomy law: a law against sex between members of the same gender.

species: a group of living things that are closely related and produce young.

spectrum: a wide range.

statute: a written law passed by a legislative body.

stereotype: an overly simple and often inaccurate picture or opinion of a person, group, or thing.

sterility: the act of being sterile, or unable to physically have children.

stigma: a mark of shame or discredit.

technology: the scientific or mechanical tools, methods, and systems used to solve a problem or do work.

terrorism: the use of violence and threats to frighten people.

testes: external reproductive organs in which sperm are produced.

tolerance: the willingness to respect or accept behavior and beliefs that are different from your own.

transgender: a person whose actual gender differs from the gender they were assigned at birth.

transphobia: intense dislike of or prejudice against transgender people.

transvestite: an older term that was used to refer to transgender people and drag performers, but is mostly considered outdated and offensive today.

tuberculosis (TB): a deadly disease of the lungs.

unconstitutional: not in agreement or accordance with a political constitution, especially the U.S. Constitution.

undermine: to damage or weaken.

uterus: an internal reproductive organ where children are conceived and gestate before being born.

Venn diagram: a diagram that uses circles to represent sets and their relationships.

vigil: a period of time, especially at night, when people stay in a place to wait for something or to give support to someone.

violate: to fail to comply with or fail to respect something.

visibility: the degree to which someone or something is noticed.

vitriol: cruel and bitter criticism.

vocational: related to skills or training needed for a specific job.

RESOURCES

BOOKS

Herman, Joanne. *Transgender Explained for Those Who Are Not.* AuthorHouse, 2009.

Testa, Rylan Jay, et al. *The Gender Quest Workbook: A Guide for Teens and Young Adults Exploring Gender Identity.* New Harbinger Publications, 2016.

Jennings, Jazz. *Being Jazz: My Life as a (Transgender) Teen.* Ember, 2017.

WEBSITES

Weiss, Suzannah. "9 Things People Get Wrong About Being Non-Binary." *Teen Vogue.* 15 February 2018. Web. 9 July 2018.
teenvogue.com/story/9-things-people-get-wrong-about-being-non-binary

Trans 101: Gender Diversity Crash Course
trans101.org.au

Genderqueer.Me: Transgender and Non-binary Resources.
genderqueer.me/2013/04/17/explaining-genderqueer-to-those-who-are-not

"Coming out as gender fluid and using gender-neutral pronouns"
All About Trans. 1 May 2014. Web. 9 July 2018.
allabouttrans.org.uk/coming-gender-fluid

QR CODE GLOSSARY

page 16: youtube.com/watch?v=loe0X5DjZX4

page 19: youtube.com/watch?v=CzcZnmYucVo

page 20: nytimes.com/1989/05/04/obituaries/christine-jorgensen-62-is-dead-was-first-to-have-a-sex-change.html

page 42: youtube.com/watch?v=SxgZNNX-v2g

page 44: blogs.presstelegram.com/outinthe562/files/2014/04/sir-lady-java-redd-foxx2.jpeg

page 52: youtube.com/watch?v=FBDO6bM0e7E

page 58: youtube.com/watch?v=XlIY91FsSc8

page 76: youtube.com/watch?v=UEPsK_axRqo

page 87: youtu.be/ZLjFGwivFtU

page 92: youtube.com/watch?v=1ZAaD1hxlm4

page 100: www2.ed.gov/about/offices/list/ocr/letters/colleague-201605-title-ix-transgender.pdf

page 105: assets2.hrc.org/files/assets/resources/A_Time_To_Act_2017_REV3.pdf

SOURCE NOTES

INTRODUCTION

1 time.com/132769/transgender-orange-is-the-new-black-laverne-cox-interview
2 abcnews.go.com/Health/MedicalMysteries/story?id=5465752&page=1
3 onlinelibrary.wiley.com/doi/10.1002/(SICI)1520-6300(200003/04)12:2%3C151::AID-AJHB1%3E3.0.CO;2-F/abstract

CHAPTER 1

1 telegraph.co.uk/films/2016/04/14/the-tragic-true-story-behind-the-danish-girl
2 thoughtco.com/lili-elbe-biography-4176321
3 biography.com/people/lili-elbe-090815
4 biography.com/people/christine-jorgensen-262758
5 nytimes.com/1989/05/04/obituaries/christine-jorgensen-62-is-dead-was-first-to-have-a-sex-change.html
6 http://outhistory.org/exhibits/show/tgi-bios/christine-jorgensen
7 revolvy.com/main/index.php?s=The+Christine+Jorgensen+Story

CHAPTER 2

1 npr.org/sections/codeswitch/2015/05/05/404459634/ladies-in-the-streets-before-stonewall-transgender-uprising-changed-lives
2 medium.com/queer-history-for-the-people/simply-sylvia-bc8d98af205d
3 workers.org/ww/1998/sylvia0702.php
4 makinggayhistory.com/podcast/episode-11-johnson-wicker
5 marshap.org
6 cnn.com/2015/06/19/us/lgbt-rights-milestones-fast-facts/index.html

CHAPTER 3

1 glaad.org/blog/timeline-look-back-history-transgender-visibility
2 aclu.org/about-aclu
3 advocate.com/politics/transgender/2012/07/23/dsm-replaces-gender-identity-disorder-gender-dysphoria
4 usatoday.com/story/news/2018/06/20/transgender-not-mental-illness-world-health-organization/717758002
5 nytimes.com/2000/05/24/nyregion/lee-brewster-57-style-guru-for-world-s-cross-dressers.html
6 pbs.org/newshour/nation/arresting-dress-timeline-anti-cross-dressing-laws-u-s
7 zagria.blogspot.com/2009/12/beth-elliott-1950-singer-activist-writer.html#.W0foa9JKg2w
8 hiv.gov/hiv-basics/overview/about-hiv-and-aids/what-are-hiv-and-aids
9 msnbc.com/msnbc/how-minneapolis-became-the-first-city-the-country-pass-trans-protections
10 ryanwhite.com/Ryans_Story.html
11 washingtonpost.com/news/arts-and-entertainment/wp/2015/12/01/a-disturbing-new-glimpse-at-the-reagan-administrations-indifference-to-aids/?utm_term=.6fb0be87f313
12 tennis.com/pro-game/2017/07/40-years-later-renee-richards-breakthrough-important-ever/68064

RESOURCES

SOURCE NOTES (CONTINUED)

CHAPTER 4

1 daily-journal.com/news/local/first-transgender-teacher-discusses-life-activism/article_5e568f24-3857-11e8-8c21-4b11331730c4.html

2 thedailybeast.com/the-trans-murder-that-started-a-movement

3 thedailybeast.com/the-trans-murder-that-started-a-movement

4 usatoday.com/story/news/nation/2015/08/16/transgender-individuals-face-high-rates--suicide-attempts/31626633

5 huffingtonpost.com/2012/11/20/transgender-flag_n_2166742.html

6 huffingtonpost.com/entry/we-have-a-navy-veteran-to-thank-for-the-transgender-pride-flag_us_5978c060e4b0e201d57a711f

CHAPTER 5

1 glsen.org/article/experiences-lgbt-youth-online

2 nytimes.com/2001/07/19/us/national-briefing-new-england-rhode-island-transgender-discrimination-banned.html

3 lgbtmap.org/equality-maps/non_discrimination_laws

4 nytimes.com/2004/03/01/us/white-house-letter-on-gay-marriage-bush-may-have-said-all-he-s-going-to.html

5 transmarch.org/about

6 aclu.org/cases/schroer-v-library-congress

7 myhusbandbetty.com/wordPressNEW/2004/06/22/gwen-araujo-trial-declared-mistrial

8 oregonencyclopedia.org/articles/rasmussen_stu_1948_/#.Wzu_B6dKg2x

9 sturasmussen.com/realityCheck.htm

10 nytimes.com/2008/08/02/us/02murder.html

CHAPTER 6

1 en.unifrance.org/movie/127/adam-est-eve

2 washingtonpost.com/lifestyle/style/should-we-forgive-friends-for-feeling-a-little-offensive-in-2016/2016/02/18/e8d47280-d0d3-11e5-b2bc-988409ee911b_story.html?utm_term=.2f426f01527c

3 io9.gizmodo.com/steven-universes-rebecca-sugar-on-how-she-expresses-her-1827624015

4 io9.gizmodo.com/steven-universe-guidebook-spills-the-secrets-of-the-cry-1704470546

CHAPTER 7

1 theatlantic.com/entertainment/archive/2014/05/laverne-cox-is-the-first-transgender-person-on-the-cover-of-time/371798

2 rollingstone.com/tv/tv-news/laverne-cox-on-oitnb-and-representing-the-trans-community-61625/

3 justice.gov/file/188671/download

4 justice.gov/opa/pr/us-departments-justice-and-education-release-joint-guidance-help-schools-ensure-civil-rights

5 freep.com/story/news/2015/06/22/fishbones-woman-speaks/71243408

6 hrc.org/resources/violence-against-the-transgender-

7 theguardian.com/global-development-professionals-network/2017/mar/01/where-are-the-most-difficult-places-in-the-world-to-be-gay-or-transgender-lgbt

INDEX

F

flags, pride, 64–66
Friends, 85, 90
Frye, Phyllis, 56, 58
FTM International, ix, 42

G

Gay Liberation Front, 33
Gazebo, 60
gender assignment, 2, 4, 31, 34, 43, 51
gender dysphoria, vii, 7, 15, 18, 45, 60, 78
gender identity
    challenges and changes.
       See challenges and changes
    culture and. *See* cultural considerations
    definition and description, 2–4
    language and, 13, 18, 29, 31,
       33, 46, 62, 91, 92, 99
    LGBTQ. *See* LGBTQ individuals;
       transgender individuals
    in media. *See* media coverage; popular media
    physical sex *vs.,* 4–5, 6, 17, 43
    pioneers and activists, vi–vii, viii–ix,
       12–22, 31–36, 42, 43–47, 78–80
    sexual orientation and, vii, ix, 5–6, 42
    timeline, vi–vii
gender identity disorder, 45, 60
gender performance, 9
Gender Public Advocacy Coalition
   (GenderPAC), 58–59
gender reassignment, vi, viii, 7, 8, 12,
   14, 15–21, 40–43, 51–52
George, 90
Girl Scouts, 98

H

Hallquist, Christine, 99
hate crimes, 59, 78
Helms, Monica, 64–66
Hester, Rita, vii, 61–63
heterosexuality, 5–6
HIV/AIDS, 49–50, 86–87
homosexuality, ix, 5–6, 37. *See*
    also LGBTQ individuals

I

International Conference on Transgender Law
   and Employment Policy, vii, 56–57
intersex individuals, 5, 6, 17, 65, 92

J

Java, Sir Lady, 43–45
The Jeffersons, 87–88
Jenner, Caitlyn, 102, 106
Johnson, Marsha P., vi, viii–ix, 33–36
Jorgensen, Christine, viii, 17–21

K

Kopriva, Karen, 60–61

L

language, 13, 18, 29, 31, 33, 46, 62, 91, 92, 99
Laverne Cox Presents: The T Word, 97–98
laws and legal status
    anti-discrimination, vi, 49, 53–54,
       56–57, 72, 74, 98–100, 103
    bathroom use, 7–8, 99, 100–103
    challenging/changing, vi–vii, 24–31,
       34, 36–37, 40–42, 44–49, 52–53,
       56–57, 67, 72, 74, 98–103
    cross-dressing, vi, 25–26, 28,
       36, 44, 46–47, 48, 56
    hate crime, 59, 78
    medical transition, 19, 40–41
    recognition of gender, 4, 8, 41, 53
    sodomy, 36, 37, 46
The Left Hand of Darkness (Le Guin), 91
legal documents, vii, 8, 16, 19, 40–42, 57
legal representation, 72–74, 75

INDEX